ONE FOR THE BOOKS

Creative Ways To Encourage
Better Book Reports

by
Joanne Richards
and
Marianne Standley

Incentive Publications, Inc.
Nashville, Tennessee

Cover and illustration adaptations by Becky Cutler

ISBN 0-86530-023-2

Copyright © 1984 Incentive Publications, Inc., Nashville, TN. All rights reserved.

Permission is hereby granted to the purchaser of one copy of ONE FOR THE BOOKS to reproduce, in sufficient quantity to meet the needs of students in one classroom, pages bearing the following statement:

©1984 Incentive Publications, Inc., Nashville, TN. All rights reserved.

TABLE OF CONTENTS

9	Walking Papers	36	A Matter of Degree
10	Hit the Jackpot!	39	Happy Medium
13	A Change in Character	40	Housewarming
15	A Charming Idea	42	Pen Money
16	Pocket-book	43	Charge!
18	A Slice of Life	45	Locker Room
20	At Opposite Poles	46	Hoe! Hoe! Hoe!
21	Play It Again	48	Sticky Fingers
23	Shopping Spree	49	Out of This World
24	Athlete's Foot	50	Just Hatched!
25	Making Ends Meet	53	Shoot for the Stars
27	A Redeeming Idea	55	Color Guard
28	In a Nutshell	57	Cross Section
30	Sweet Talk	58	Hold Your Horses
31	Greetings!	61	Party Line
33	Sure Cure	63	Rain or Shine
35	Keyed Up	64	Fan-tastic!

66	Jump to a Conclusion	100	Make a Beeline
68	Get the Picture?	103	Head Start
71	Preserve It!	105	APPENDIX
72	Strut Your Stuff	106	Critic's Choice
74	A to Z	109	Planning and Evaluation
75	Masquerade	110	Make It Snappy
77	Weigh Your Words	111	Sound Effects
81	To the Nth Degree	111	Show Off
83	Sew Bee It!	112	Writer's Cramp
85	Single File	114	Looking Back
86	Happy Landings	114	Smart Cookie
88	Shoot Out	115	Scavenger Hunt
90	One Good Turn	115	Reading Relay
91	Something's Fishy	116	Check It Out!
93	If the Shoe Fits	117	Mark My Word
94	Ticket-Taker	118	Holiday Ideas and More
96	Pot Luck	121	Reminders
97	Abracadabra	122	Bookmarks
99	Toast of the Town	126	Corner a Good Book

INTRODUCTION

ONE FOR THE BOOKS is a teacher/student resource book created to liven up book reporting. The directions for each activity are easy to understand and the finished products are both unique and attractive.

The main purpose of ONE FOR THE BOOKS is to offer creative approaches to an ordinarily traditional format. By introducing different ideas in book reporting, students can discover both the fun of reading and the satisfaction of successfully completing a task.

It would be helpful before using this book, for teachers to become familiar with the kinds of books being read by students and the types of activities available in ONE FOR THE BOOKS.

Happy Reading!

WALKING PAPERS

In most books, the main character leads the reader to another character. Make a set of paper dolls to show the characters from your book.

1. Think of the characters in your book. Cut a set of paper dolls about five to six inches tall. Be sure you have enough for the main characters and his or her friends and enemies.

2. On the front of each paper doll, illustrate a character from the book. Begin with the main character. Write the character's name across the front of the doll.

3. On the back of each doll, tell what part that character played in the story. Be sure to include who, what, where, when and why.

4. Decorate a box to show the main setting of the story. Label the front of the box with _____ 's House. Write your name on the inside of the box lid.

5. Fold the dolls together and place them inside the box.

HIT THE JACKPOT

Have you read a book that's really a winner? Make this slot machine and hit the jackpot with a book project!

1. Use a detergent or cereal box for the slot machine. Cover the box with bright wrapping paper or shelf paper.

2. Turn the box upside down so that the pouring spout is at your bottom right. Slit the paper so that the coins can come out for viewing. (See illustration A.)

3. Make a slit in the box lid about three inches long. Coins will be deposited here. (See illustration A.)

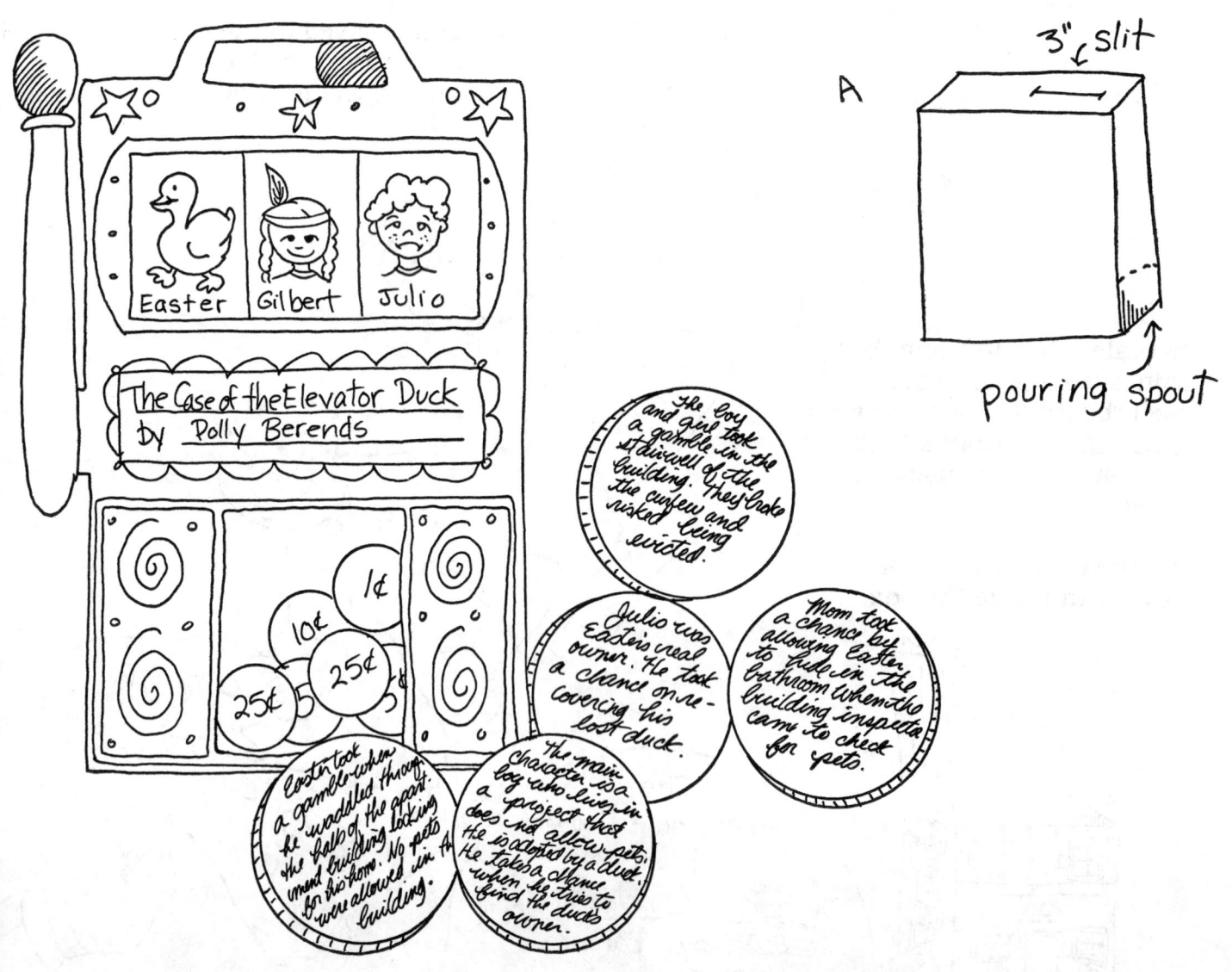

4. Draw pictures of the three main characters from your book or cut out pictures from a magazine. Glue the pictures in the rectangles at the top of the slot machine front. (See illustration.)

5. Color the remainder of the slot machine front. Cut it out and glue it to the box front.

6. Using the coin pattern and yellow or gold construction paper, make one coin for each character in your book.

7. Write the character's name on one side of each coin. On the other side, tell how that character took a chance, won or lost in the story.

8. Write the title of the book and the author's name on the lines of the slot machine front.

9. Drop the coins inside the slit in the box lid.

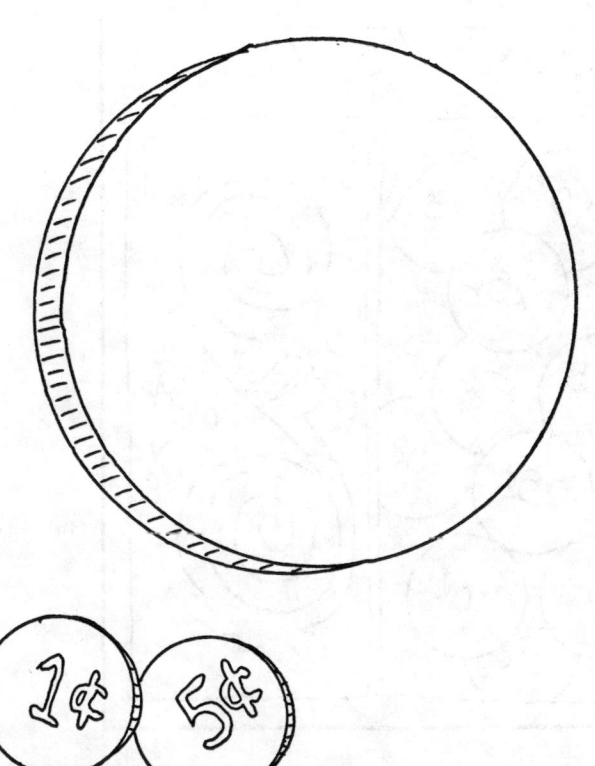

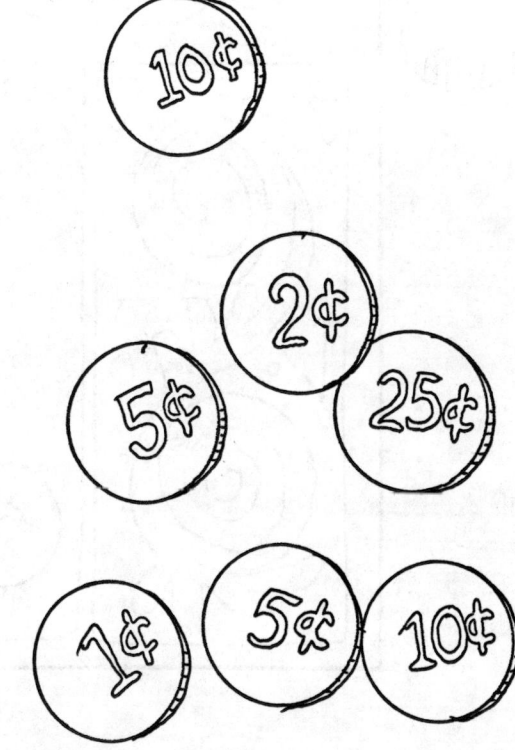

©1984 INCENTIVE PUBLICATIONS, Inc., Nashville, TN. All rights reserved.

A CHANGE IN CHARACTER

Characters in a book change and grow as a story progresses. Help your characters come out of their cocoons by making a butterfly mobile for the characters in your book.

1. Fold a piece of 11 x 14 inch construction paper in half. Place the butterfly pattern on the fold and trace around it. Make one butterfly for each character in your book and one for the book title and author.

2. Cut out the inside of each wing along the dotted lines. Do not cut along the fold.

3. Open the butterfly at the fold. Insert a piece of notebook paper in the space between the front and the back of the butterfly.

4. Close the butterfly with the paper inside and staple at the "X." Trim away the excess notebook paper.

5. On the left wing, tell how the character appeared and behaved at the beginning of the book. On the right wing, explain how the character had changed by the end of the book. Be sure to tell what caused the change(s).

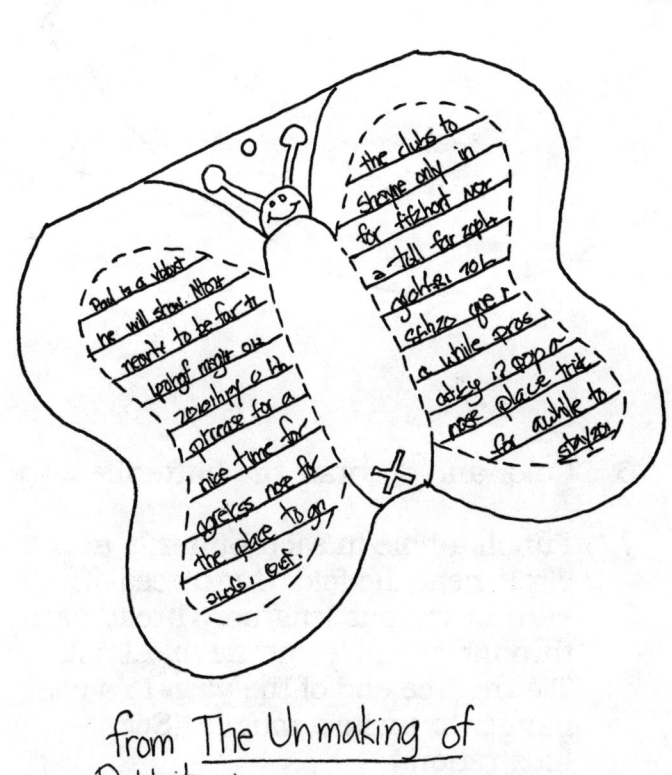

from *The Unmaking of Rabbit* by Constance Greene

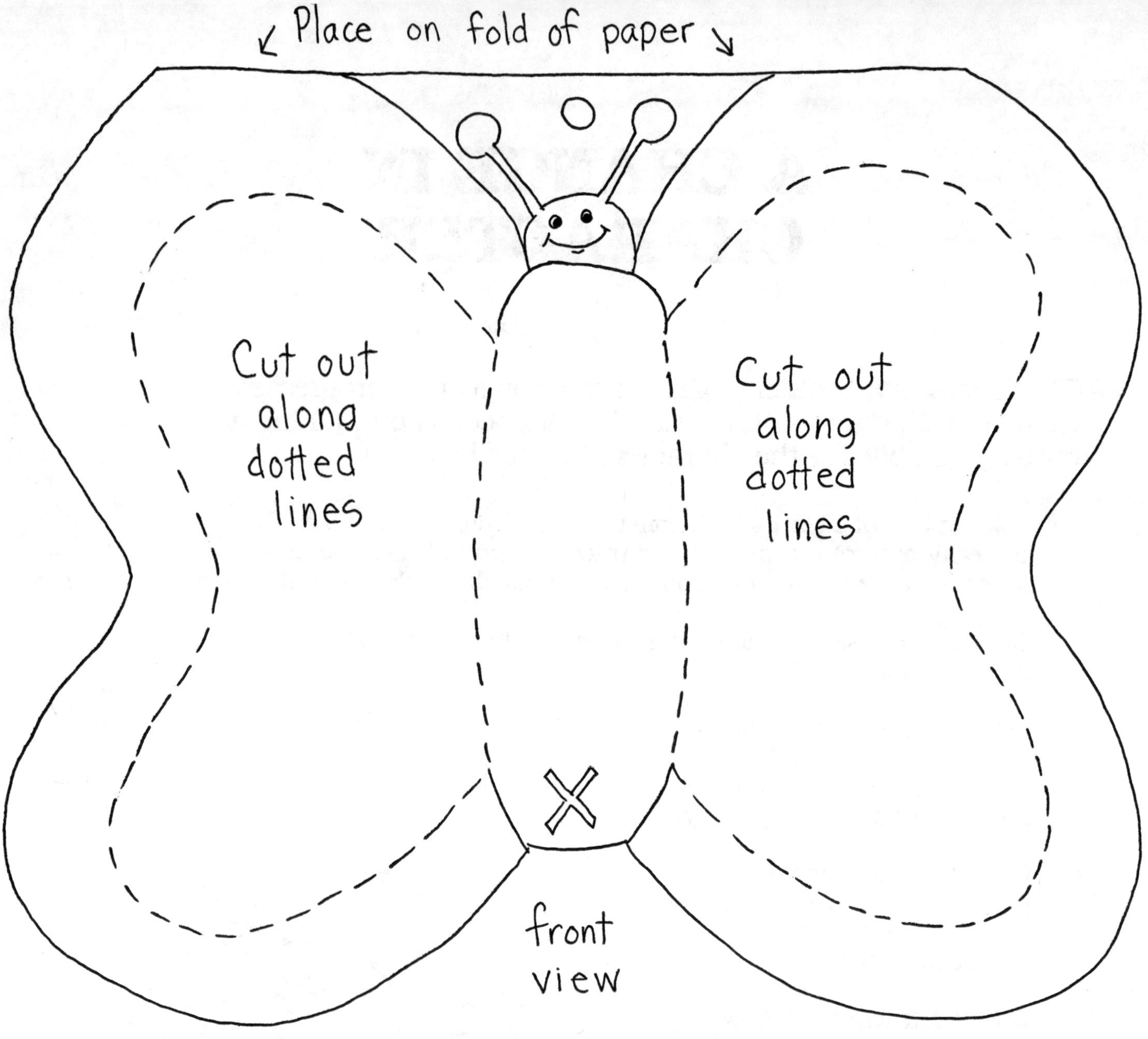

← Place on fold of paper →

Cut out along dotted lines

Cut out along dotted lines

front view

6. Color and decorate the butterflies.

7. Punch a hole in each butterfly at the circle near the fold. Cut pieces of yarn in various lengths. Thread yarn through the hole and tie in a knot. Tie the free end of the yarn to a coat hanger to make a mobile. (See illustration.)

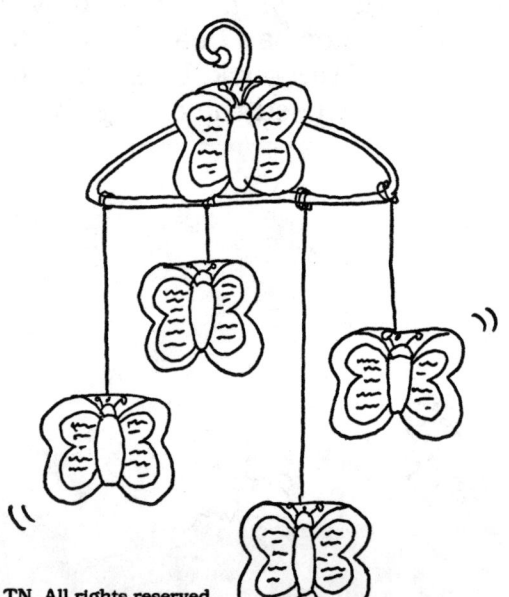

©1984 INCENTIVE PUBLICATIONS, Inc., Nashville, TN. All rights reserved.

14

A CHARMING IDEA

Create a charm bracelet to remember your book by. Each charm symbolizes either characters, setting or events from the plot.

1. Trace your own hand and forearm on a piece of posterboard.

2. Make a bracelet of posterboard large enough to encircle the arm. Do not connect the ends of the bracelet yet.

3. Make eight to ten charms from posterboard, construction paper or tagboard. These charms should illustrate the characters, setting and plot. (See illustration.)

4. On the back of each charm, tell how it symbolizes something from the book.

5. Punch holes in the bracelet — one for each charm. Punch a hole in the top of each charm. Connect the charms to the bracelet with yarn, string or ribbon.

6. Fit the bracelet around the wrist and staple the ends of the bracelet together.

7. Decorate the hand with nail polish and rings.

8. Write the book title and author on the forearm.

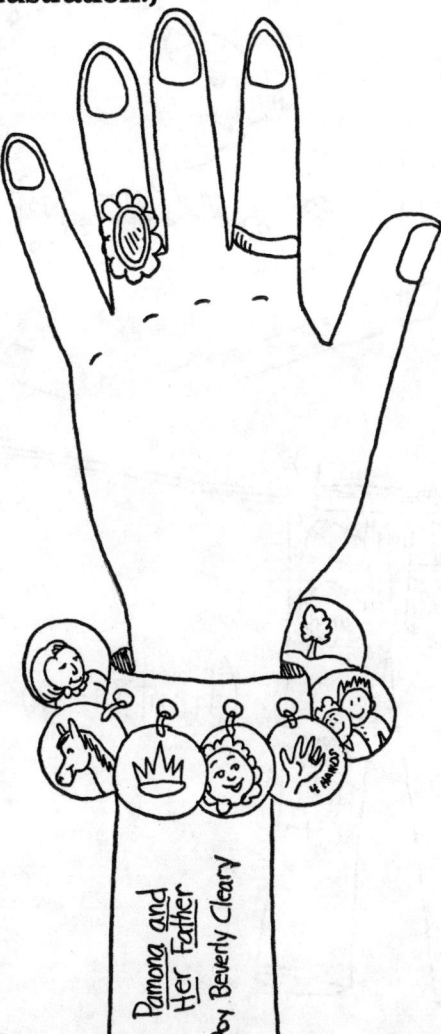

POCKET-BOOK

Line your pockets with a handkerchief that tells about your book! It's time to design pockets for the characters you read about.

1. Using the pocket pattern and light blue construction paper, trace a pocket for each important character or scene in your book.

2. Draw the characters or setting on the pocket or use pictures from a magazine. Decorate the pocket with top stitching. (See illustration.)

3. Using scrap fabric, cut an eight-inch square "handkerchief" for each pocket. Use a marker to briefly describe each character or scene.

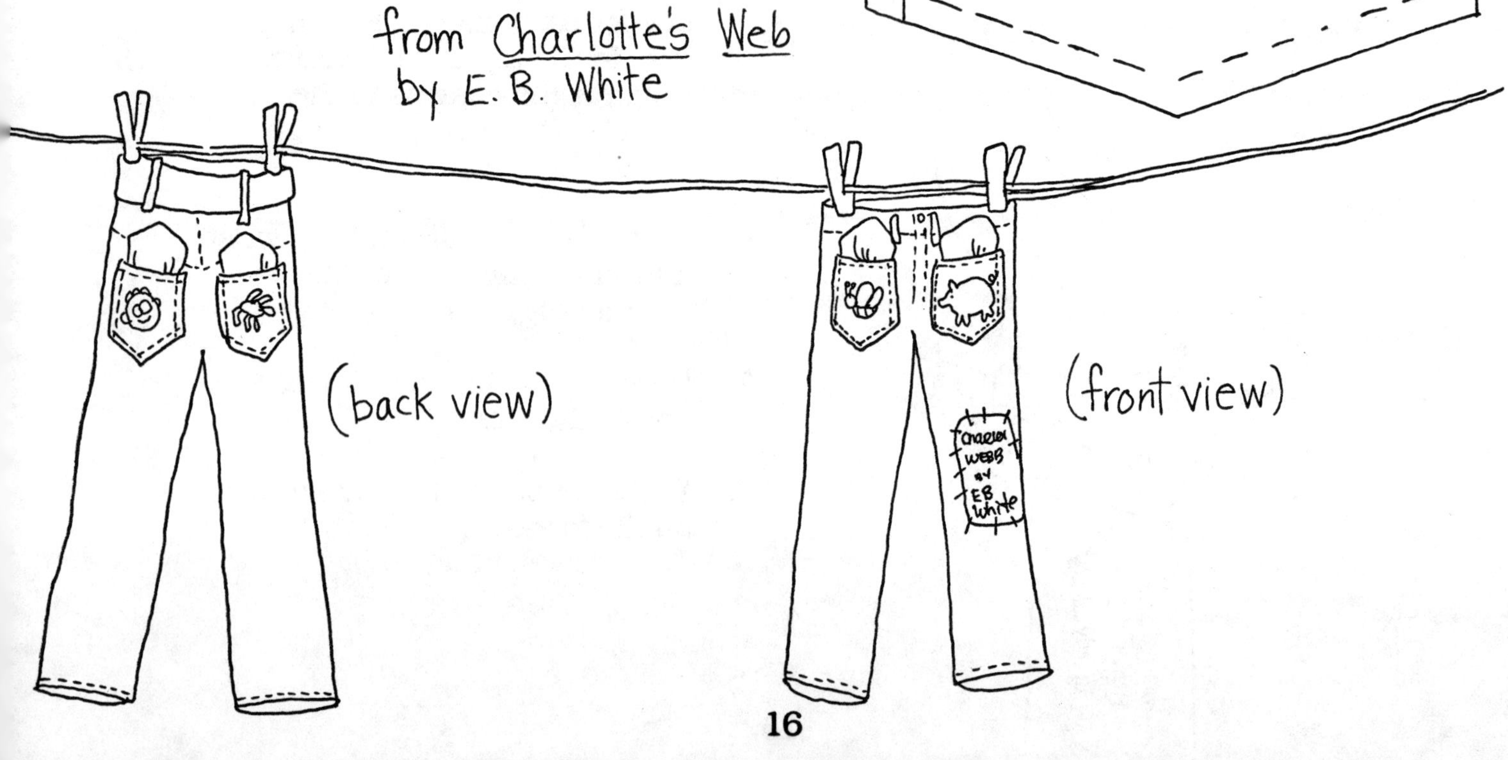

from *Charlotte's Web* by E. B. White

(back view)   (front view)

4. Cut out pockets and staple, stitch or glue them to the pockets of an old pair of blue jeans. Place each "handkerchief" in its appropriate pocket.

5. Design a knee patch for the title and author of the book. Staple, stitch or glue it in place.

6. Hang your jeans from a clothesline in the classroom.

A SLICE OF LIFE

Reading a biography? Serve up the people and events in a pie that illustrates the life of the main character.

1. Using the pattern, make six pie slices from tan construction paper for the bottom crust. On each slice, write a person or event important to the main character. Tape each slice to the inside of a nine-inch aluminum pie pan. Crease each slice at the dotted line to fit the inside of the pan. (See illustration A.)

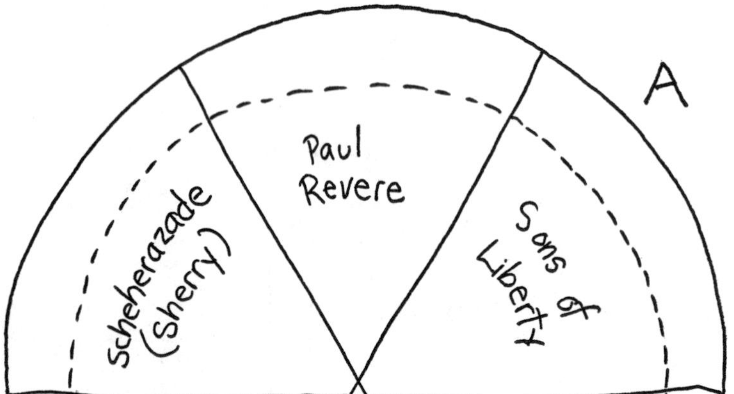

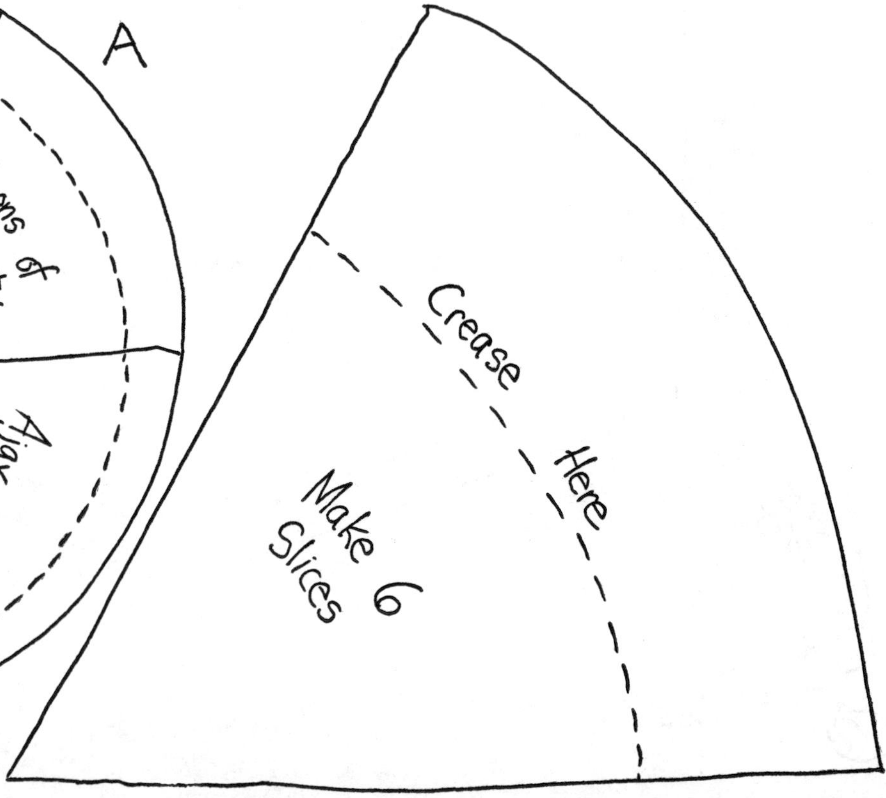

©1984 Incentive Publications, Inc., Nashville, TN. All rights reserved.

2. Trace the bottom of the aluminum pie pan on construction paper of an appropriate color for your pie filling (blue for blueberry, yellow for lemon). Cut out the filling and explain the people or events written about the bottom crust. Fit into the pan over the crust. (See illustration B.)

3. Turn the aluminum pie pan over and trace around the rim on a piece of tan construction paper. This is the top crust. Write the name of the book and author on the crust. Decorate the top to look like a pie. Place the top crust on top of the pie pan. Hinge the rim of the top crust to the pan with a piece of tape. (See illustration C.)

AT OPPOSITE POLES

Some book characters have personalities that draw you to them. Others are just the opposite — they repel the reader. Use this magnetic idea to show how the characters in your book act.

1. Make a magnet, eight to ten inches high, out of posterboard or tagboard. Put a "+" for positively behaving characters at the end of one pole and a "−" for negatively behaving characters at the end of the other pole.

2. Draw each character on a 3 x 5 inch card or use pictures from magazines.

3. On the back of each card, explain the positive or negative behavior of the character.

4. Punch a hole in the top of each card and in the top of the magnet. Punch holes in the poles of the magnet too — one for each character. (See illustration.)

5. Write the title and author of the book on the arch of the magnet.

6. Cut several lengths of yarn. Attach the cards to the magnet with the pieces of yarn. Also attach a length of yarn to the top hole of the magnet.

7. Hang your magnet as a mobile.

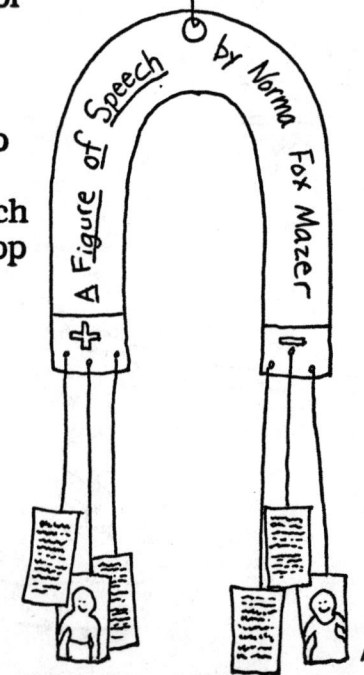

20

Go on record with a good book! Make this one a song to remember with records dedicated to your book and an album cover that says it all!

PLAY IT AGAIN

1. Use a legal-sized manila folder for the album cover. Cut off the tabs.

2. Using ¾-inch transparent or colored tape, tape the top of the folder shut. Fold the folder in half. (See illustration A.) There should now be openings at both ends of the folder to house the records.

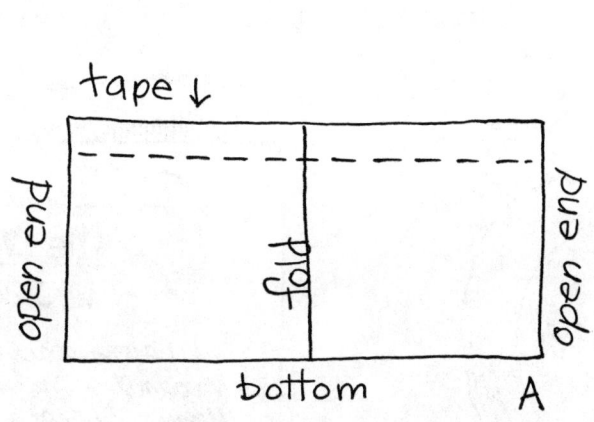

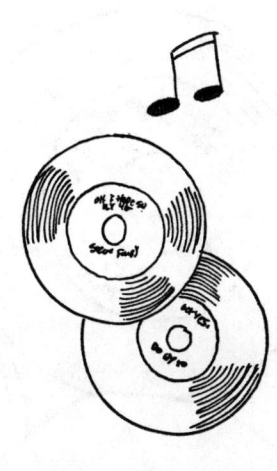

3. Make two 45 r.p.m. records (approximately seven inches in diameter) from black posterboard or construction paper. Make four record labels (three inches in diameter) from brightly colored construction paper.

4. On the inside of the album, draw pictures of the characters or use magazine pictures. Label each picture with the character's name.

5. On the album front, make a collage of the book's setting or theme. Use magazine pictures or draw your own pictures with markers.

6. On the album back, write the name and author of the book, give a brief summary of the book and name the records enclosed in the album.

7. Think of four songs whose titles and messages describe the characters and events from the book. On each record label, write a song title and the name of the person who made the song famous.

8. Glue the labels on the records and place one record in each album pocket.

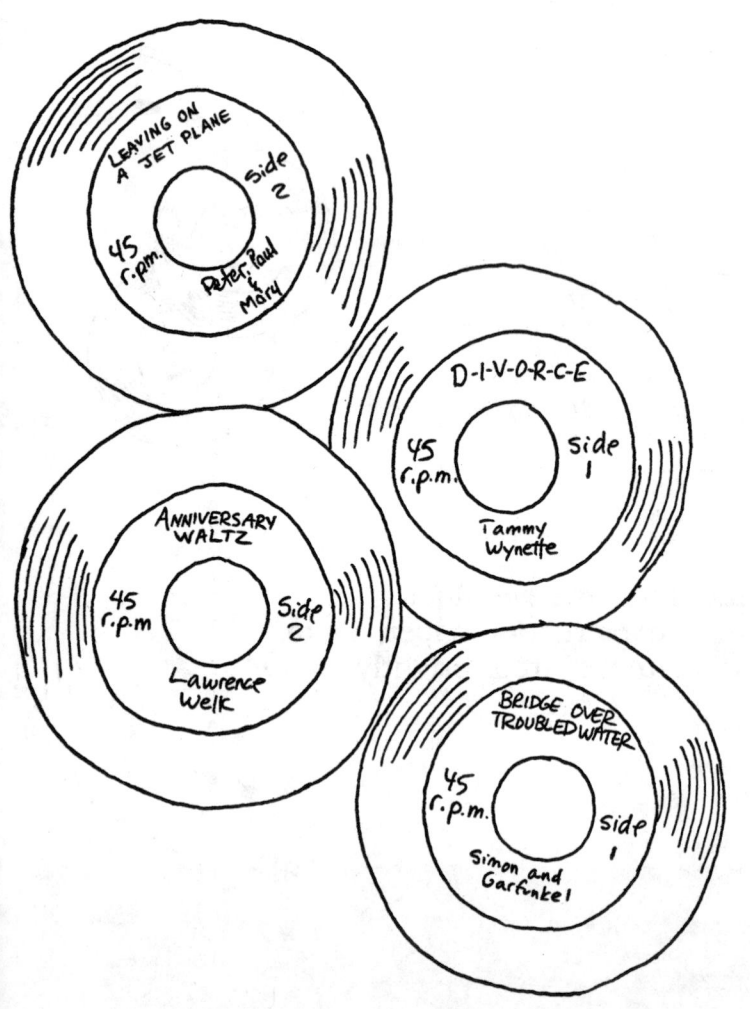

22

SHOPPING SPREE

Let's go on a shopping spree with the characters in your book.

1. Decorate a large paper bag or plain shopping bag with a collage of the important events from your book.

2. Write a name on the front of the bag that would be a suitable store name for the book.

3. Collect objects or pictures of objects that have meaning in the story. Mount each picture on posterboard or tagboard.

4. On the back of each picture, explain its significance in the story. If a real object is used, make a small tag for this purpose.

5. Place all pictures and/or objects in the shopping bag.

from Roald Dahl's *Charlie and the Chocolate Factory*

ATHLETE'S FOOT

Some books really sock it to you! Jog your memory and write a report about your sports book.

1. Trace or draw your bare foot and leg up to your knee on posterboard. Make one for each character or sports figure in your book.

2. Write the character's name on the foot. Use the leg to tell what part that character played in the book. (See illustration.)

3. Make two bands of colored construction paper to go around the bands of an athletic sock. On one paper band, write the title of the book. On the other paper band, write the author's name. Staple the construction paper bands to an athletic sock so that they cover the colored bands on the sock.

4. Insert all the feet into an athletic sock.

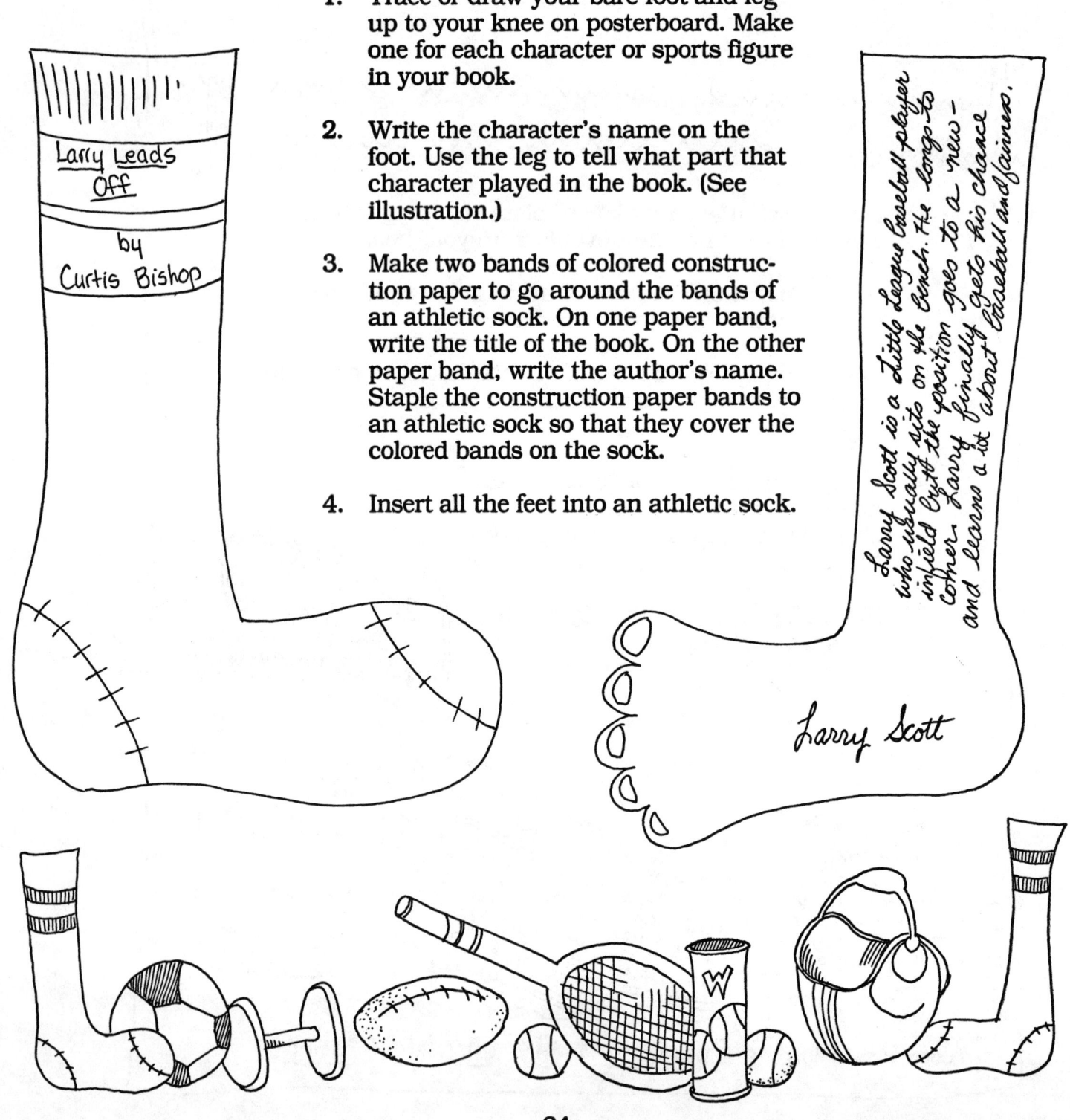

MAKING ENDS MEET

If you've been short on ideas for that book of stories, plays or poetry, tie up loose ends with bookends!

1. For each favorite story, play or poem in your book, use an empty food box (gelatin, macaroni, cereal) to represent the books. Cut the top, bottom and one side (not front, or remaining side) from the boxes.

2. Cover the boxes with construction paper. Write the title and author of the story, play or poem on the "books'" spines. Decorate the front of each book like a book jacket.

3. Write a brief summary of the story, play or poem. Secure the summary inside the front cover of the book. Be sure to include who, what, where, when and why.

4. To make the bookends, use a piece of posterboard that measures 30 x 6 inches. Fold the posterboard at each end. (See illustration A.) Leave a three-inch length at each end.

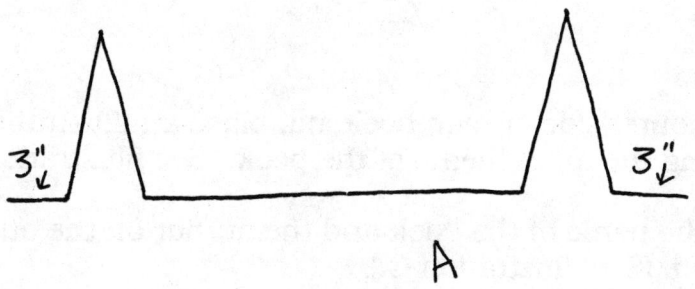

A

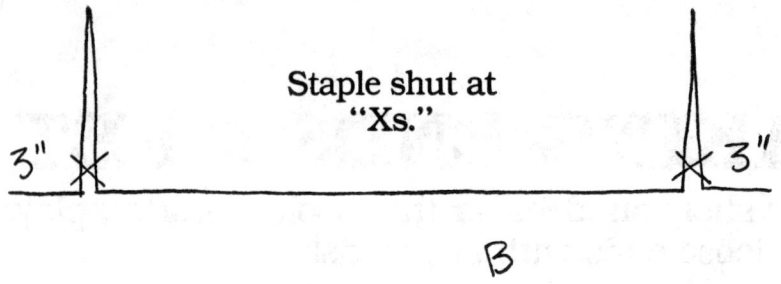

B

5. Staple upright pieces together at the bottom of the fold. Do this at each end. (See illustration B.)

C

6. On the outer side of each bookend, place an illustration or collage depicting the main theme of the book. (See illustration C.)

7. Write the name of the book and the author on the outer base of each bookend. (See illustration C.)

8. Place the food-box books between the bookends and display.

A REDEEMING IDEA

This idea is good for one book activity when presented to the teacher. Only one coupon book per reader, please.

1. The main character in your book would like to redeem coupons for different things. Make a different colored 4 x 6 inch coupon for each item to be redeemed.

2. Also make a 4 x 6 inch page showing to whom the coupon book has been issued.

3. Decorate each page appropriately. (See illustration.)

4. Make a decorative front and back cover for the coupons from tagboard or posterboard. Write the name of the book and the author on the cover. Staple cover, issue page and coupons together.

IN A NUTSHELL

Each character in a book contributes to the main part of the story. Use this idea with a book you are nuts about!

1. Make a peanut from the pattern for each character in your book.

2. Write the character's name at the top of the shell.

3. Briefly, in a nutshell, write the main contribution each character made to the story's plot on the front and back of the peanut.

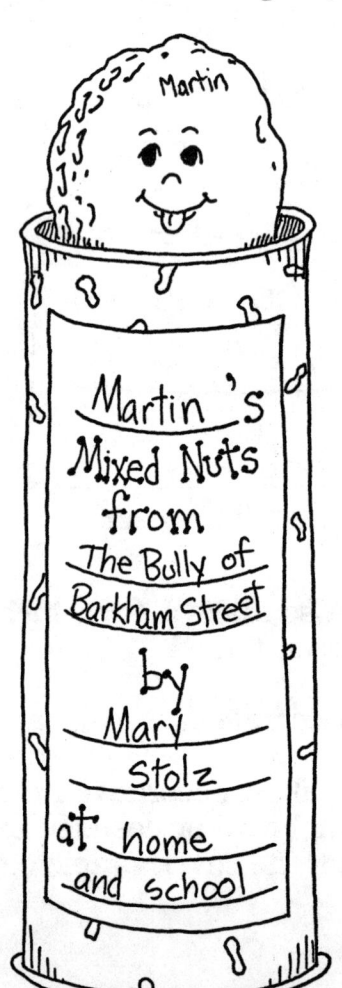

4. Decorate a tall potato chip can.

5. Using the label, fill in the blanks with information from the book.

6. Place all finished peanuts in the decorated can.

_____'s
Mixed Nuts from
_____
_____
by
_____
_____
at
_____

main character
title
author
setting

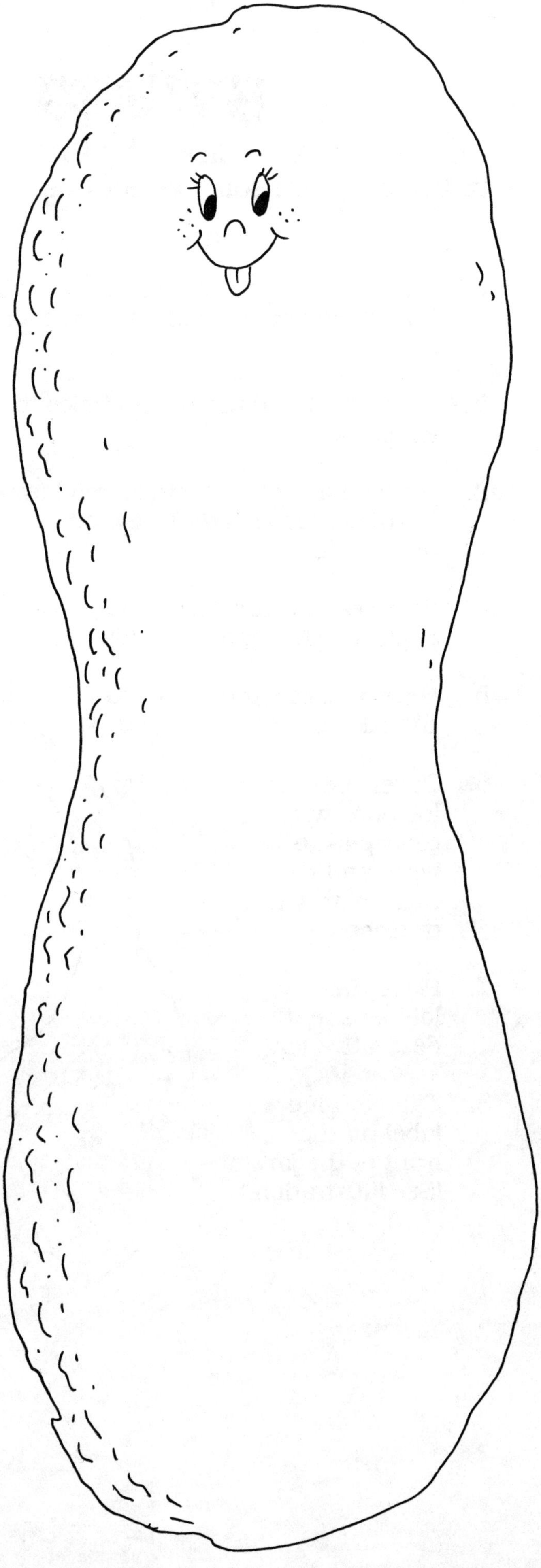

©1984 Incentive Publications, Inc., Nashville, TN. All rights reserved.

SWEET TALK

Characters can be licked by their situations or can become unlickable! Use some sweet talk to tell your book's tale.

1. Cut circles approximately three inches in diameter from pastel paper. Cut one circle for each major character.

2. Decorate the fronts of the circles to resemble lollipops.

3. On the back of each circle, tell how each character was nearly licked or unlickable.

4. Write each character's name on a popsicle stick or tongue depressor.

5. Glue or staple the circles to the sticks.

6. Cover the lollipops with clear plastic wrap and tie them with yarn or ribbon.

7. Place the lollipops in a decorative jar.

8. Tape or glue a label on the front of the jar. (See illustration.)

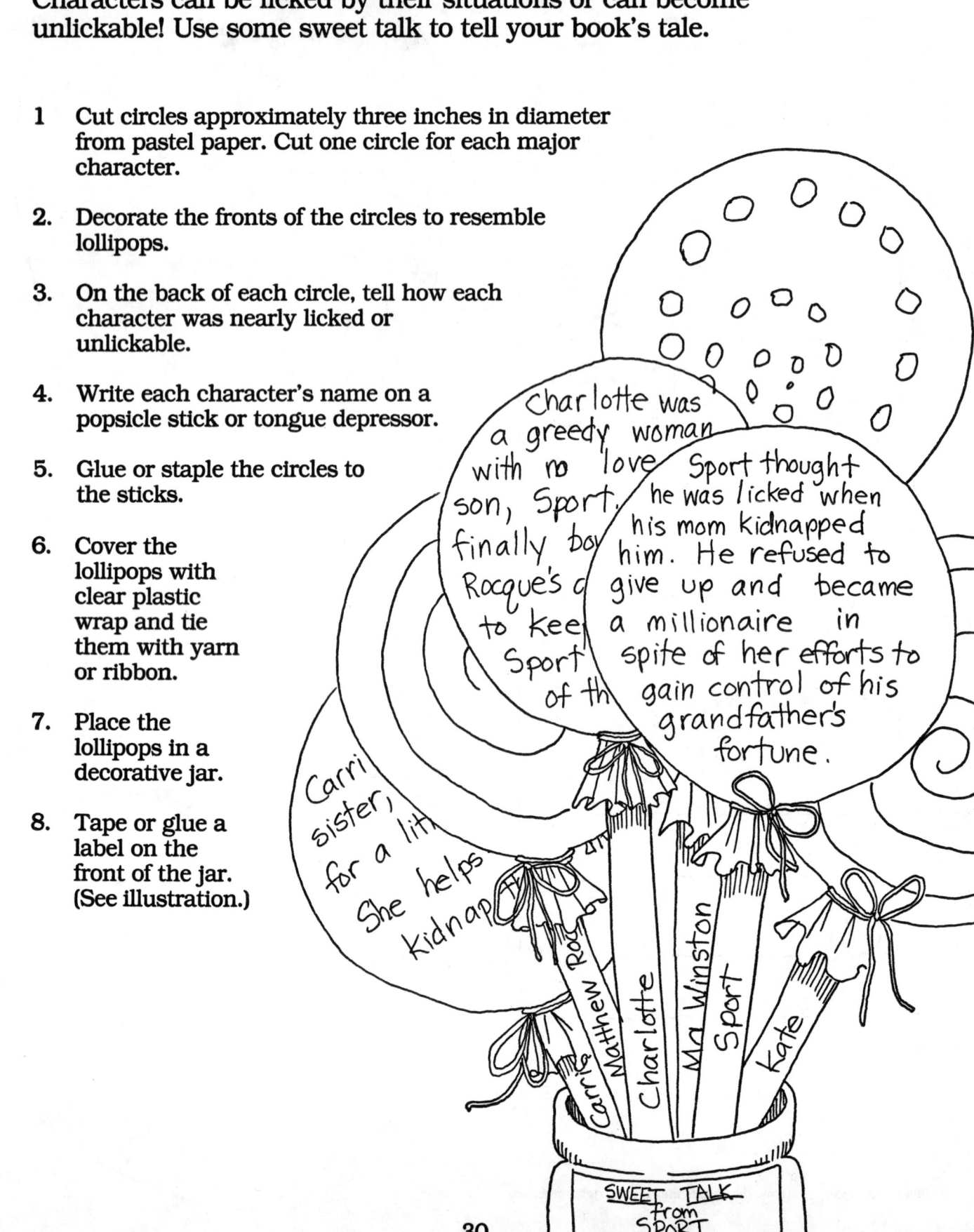

GREETINGS!

Make your book a special occasion! These greeting cards can mark all the noteworthy events in the characters' lives.

1. For each important event in your book, design an appropriate greeting card, invitation or announcement:

    birthday
    get well
    sympathy
    thank you
    invitations (party, wedding, shower)
    holidays
    bon voyage
    friendship
    announcements (birth, marriage)
    special events (Bar Mitzvah, Communion)
    graduation
    Father's Day and Mother's Day
    anniversary

2. Inside each card, write a message appropriate to the event.

3. Make an envelope for each card. Address each envelope and write a return address.

4. Staple the open top of a half-gallon milk carton shut. (See illustration on following page.)

5. Spray paint the carton blue.

6. Glue a two-inch-wide white strip around the middle of the carton. Write "U.S. MAIL" on the strip. (See illustration.)

31

7. Make a three-sided opening in the top of the carton. The opening should measure 3 x 5 inches. (See illustration.)

8. Make a handle from posterboard and staple it to the flap on the carton.

9. Write the book title and its author on a 3 x 5 inch index card. Attach the card to the bottom front of the mailbox.

10. Place the greeting cards in the mailbox.

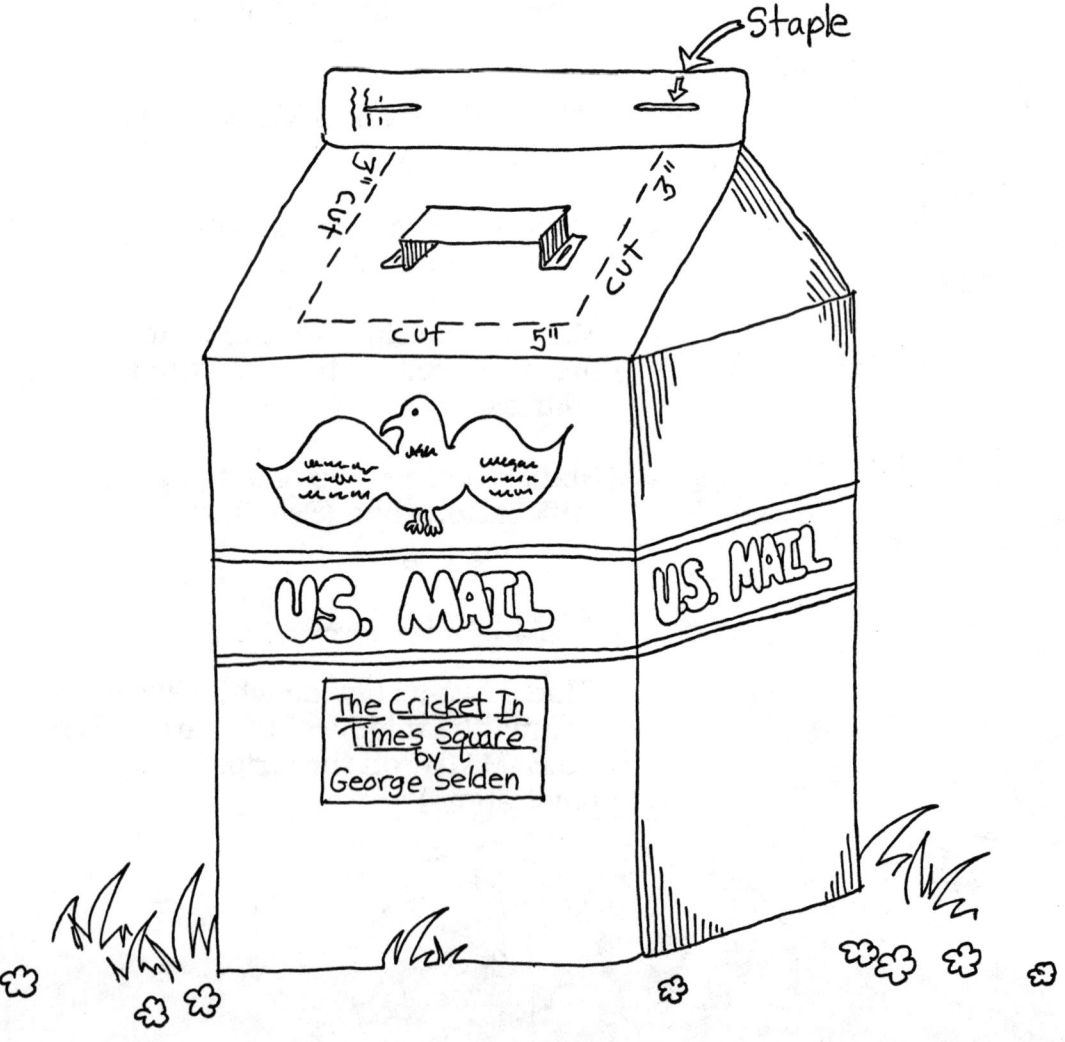

SURE CURE

If book reports have a case of the "blahs" in your classroom, try this remedy. It's just what the doctor ordered!

1. Use a cigar or school box for the medicine cabinet. Cover the top and sides with construction paper of a solid color.

2. Cut a piece of aluminum foil one inch smaller than the box lid and use it as a mirror for the medicine chest. Glue the mirror to the outside front of the box.

3. Draw a picture of the book's main character (view from shoulders up) and glue it to the top of the foil to resemble a reflection. (See illustration.)

4. Glue a cap from a lotion bottle or tube to the front top of the box as a handle.

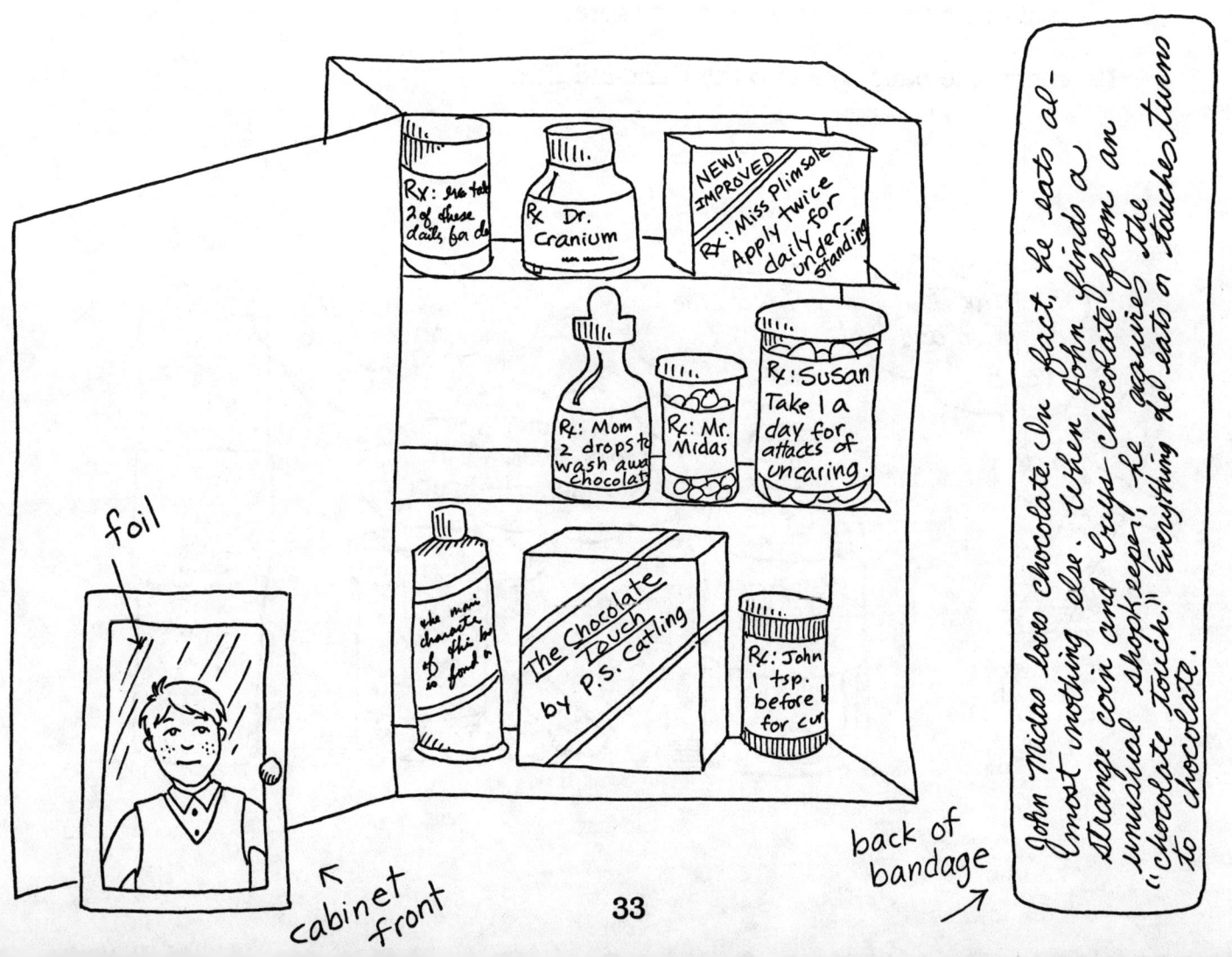

5. Place one small plastic hook with peel-and-stick backing on a side wall of the medicine chest. (See illustration.) Hang a real or construction paper toothbrush on the hook.

6. Draw two shelves on the inside back wall of the medicine cabinet.

7. Make pill bottles, boxes and tubes from construction paper.

8. Make prescription labels for each container. Write the name of a character and the directions for taking the remedy on each label. Be sure to mention what needs to be remedied. Attach the labels to the containers.

9. Place a white peel-and-stick label on the front of a Band-aid box. Write the name of the book and the author on the label.

10. Make bandages from construction paper for the characters in the book. On the back of each bandage, explain why the character needs a remedy.

11. Decorate the front of each construction paper bandage to resemble a real one or place a real bandage there.

12. Insert the bandages into the Band-aid box.

KEYED UP

Unlock reading pleasure with these keys to a good book!

1. Make keys that the characters in your book would use to unlock settings in the story or solutions to their problems.

2. On the back of each key, write the name of the character who would use it and the place or the problem it would unlock.

3. Place all of the keys on a chain or binder ring.

4. On a decorative tag, write the book title and the author's name. Place this tag on the key ring.

A MATTER OF DEGREE

If your readers are sleeping through their books, count on these sheep to wake them up! Your kids will graduate with flying colors in two shakes of a lamb's "tale"!

1. Use the pattern to make a "sheepskin" for each major character who learned something of value.

2. Write what the character learned on the sheepskin. Sign the character's name on the last line. (See illustration A.)

3. Roll each sheepskin to resemble a diploma and tie with ribbon or yarn.

4. Fill in the blanks on the large diploma with the author's name, the book title and your name and date. (See illustration B.)

5. Cut out the diploma and wrap it around a potato chip can. Secure the diploma in place with tape.

6. Place the sheepskins in the can. Tie a ribbon around the can.

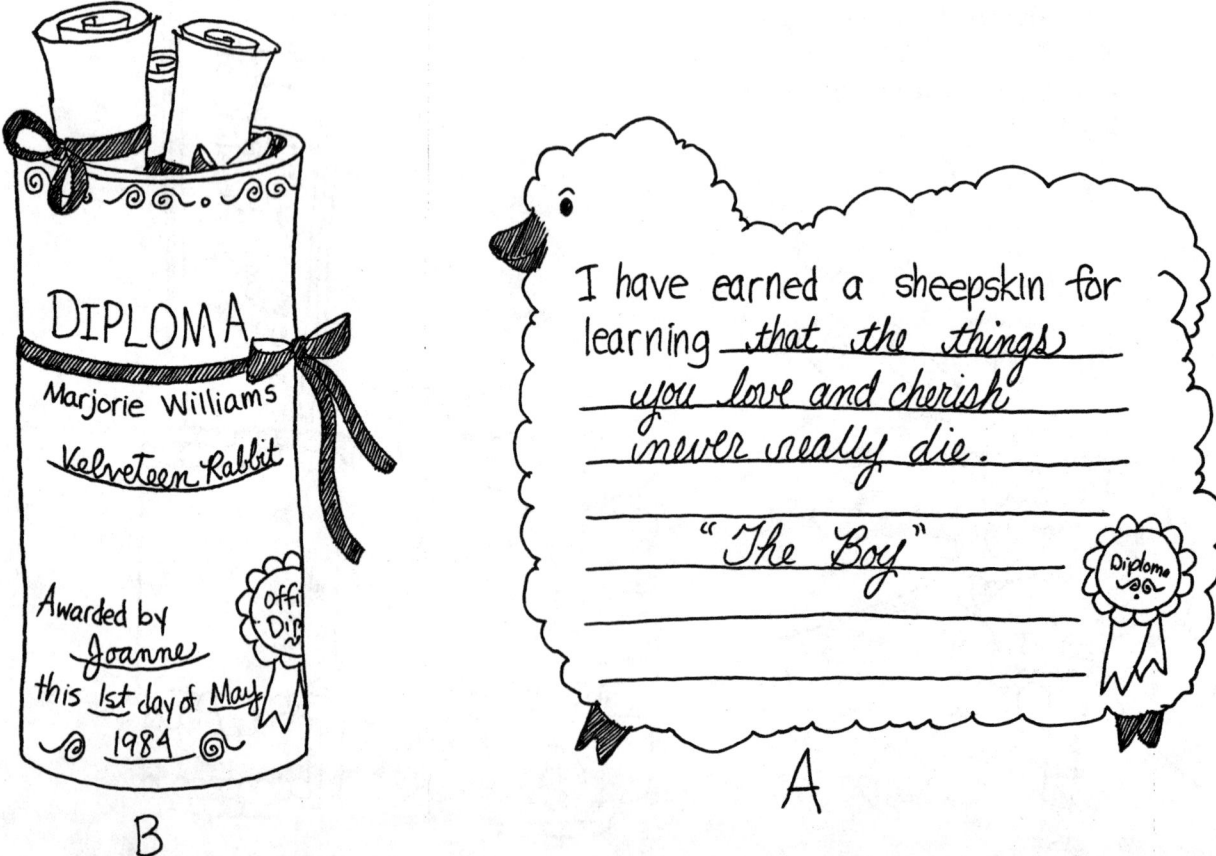

I have earned a sheepskin for learning _____
_____
_____
_____
_____

I have earned a sheepskin for learning _____
_____
_____
_____
_____

Diploma

_____ has earned this diploma for writing _____

Official Seal

Awarded by _____
on this _____ day of _____,
198__.

©1984 Incentive Publications, Inc., Nashville, TN. All rights reserved.

HAPPY MEDIUM

You don't need a crystal ball to recognize a good book, but this idea might be magical for your students.

1. Make symbols two inches in size for each important event or character in your book.

2. Pin the symbols on a four to six inch Styrofoam ball.

3. Cover the ball with clear plastic wrap. Gather the wrap beneath the ball and draw it taut with tape. Clip off the excess wrap.

4. Use a two-and-one-half inch lid from a plastic spray can for the crystal ball holder. Place the name and author of the book on the side of the lid. (See illustration.)

5. Make a card for each symbol on the ball. Write the significance of the symbol on the back of the card.

HOUSEWARMING

This idea is for a book that is good enough to write home about! Recreate the setting of your book by making the whole neighborhood.

1. Use a square tissue box, 4½ x 4½ inches, for each building. One-story buildings can be made by using only the top half of the box.

2. Make a roof for each building from a piece of posterboard, 4½ x 8 inches. Fold the roof in half lengthwise. Make a one-and-one-half inch slit in the middle of the fold. (See illustration A.)

3. Draw a chimney on one side of the roof beneath the slit.

4. Make slits along two opposing sides of the top of the tissue box. (See illustration B.)

5. Cover the box with construction paper and decorate it to resemble a house, store, school, building or castle.

6. Insert the edges of the roof into the slits at the top of the box.

guppies, they soon multiplied. The Huggins' house was like a giant aquarium
↑ back

Henry always came out on top when he was involved in sticky situations that he couldn't handle. When he bought a pair of
front ↑

A — slit

THE HUGGINS'

B — slit along dotted lines

40

7. Make "smoke" from posterboard with the base measuring 2½ x 1½ inches. (See illustration C.)

8. Write a brief account of the important events that occurred in the house or building on the smoke.

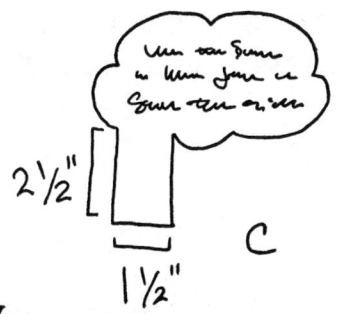

9. Insert the "smoke" into the appropriate chimney.

10. Group the houses or buildings on a piece of posterboard to form a neighborhood. (See illustration D.)

11. Make a street sign with the name of the book and the author on it. Place the sign on a corner of the neighborhood.

PEN MONEY

You'll want to bank on this book report idea for characters who will cash in on savings.

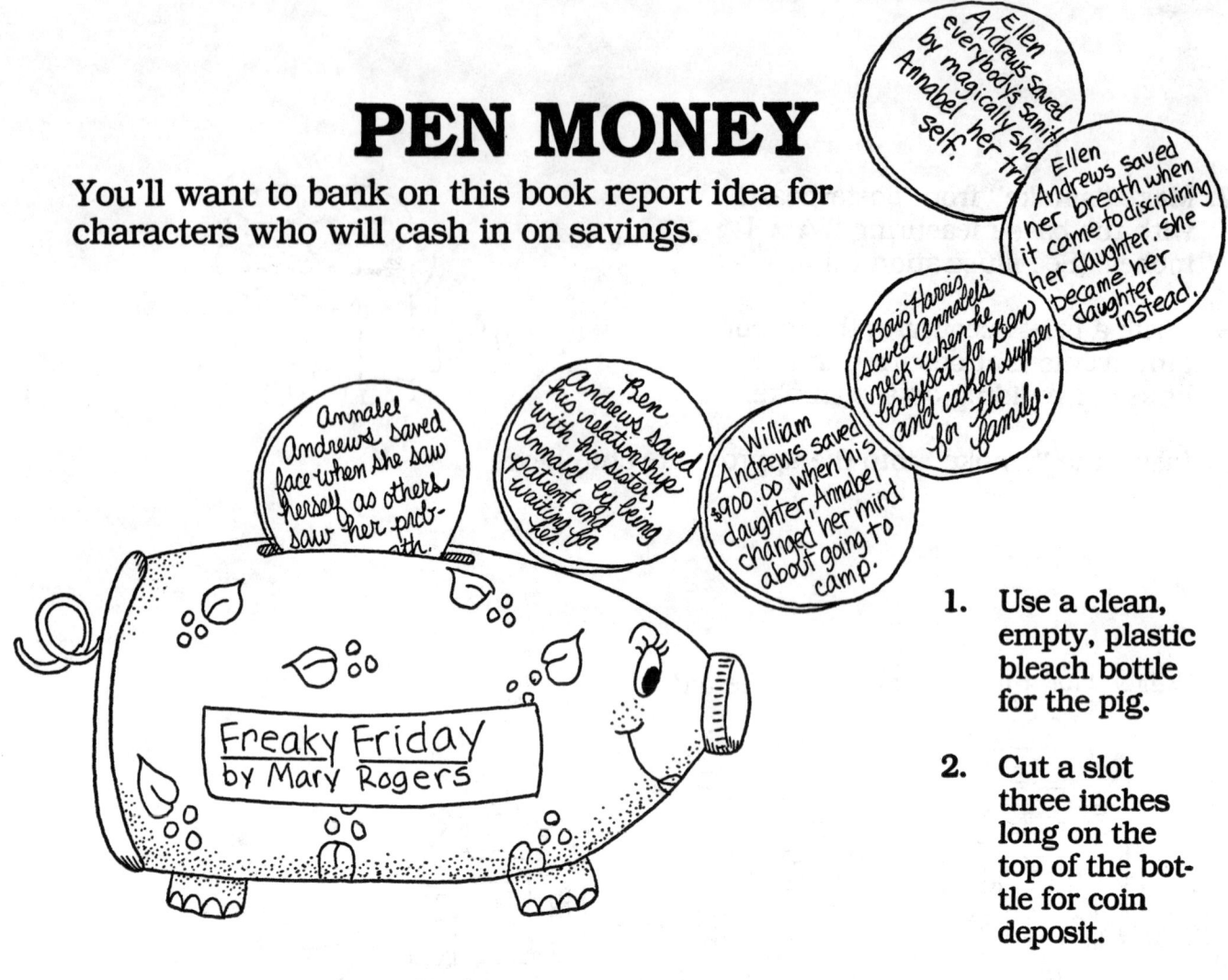

Coin annotations (on piggy bank illustration):

- Ellen Andrews saved everybody's sanity by magically showing Annabel her true self.
- Ellen Andrews saved her breath when it came to disciplining her daughter. She became her daughter instead.
- Boris Harris saved Annabel's neck when he babysat for Ben and cooked supper for the family.
- William Andrews saved $900.00 when his daughter, Annabel, changed her mind about going to camp.
- Ben Andrews saved his relationship with his sister, Annabel, by being patient and waiting for her.
- Annabel Andrews saved face when she saw herself as others saw her problems.

Label on pig: Freaky Friday by Mary Rogers

1. Use a clean, empty, plastic bleach bottle for the pig.

2. Cut a slot three inches long on the top of the bottle for coin deposit.

3. Decorate the bottle with permanent felt tip markers to look like a piggy bank. Write the name of the book and the author on a label and place it on the side of the piggy bank.

4. Insert a coiled pipe cleaner in the rear of the bottle for the pig's tail.

5. On the side of the bottle opposite the slot, cut a three-sided opening approximately 2 x 3 inches. Coins may be removed from this opening.

6. Use the coin pattern from HIT THE JACKPOT to make coins appropriate for the characters in the book. You may want to tell how characters:

saved the day	saved a life
saved face	saved for a rainy day
saved time	saved money
saved someone's neck	saved their breath
had saving grace	

7. Insert the coins into the piggy bank.

42

CHARGE!

You'll charge into a good book report when you help the characters meet their needs with their own credit cards!

1. Use a letter-sized manila folder to make a billfold, charge cards and an I.D. card.

2. With the folder closed, cut a wallet shape, 4 x 8 inches. (See illustration A.)

3. From the remainder of the folder, cut another single piece, 4 x 8 inches.

4. Cut credit card shapes, 2½ x 3¾ inches. Make one credit card for each main character.

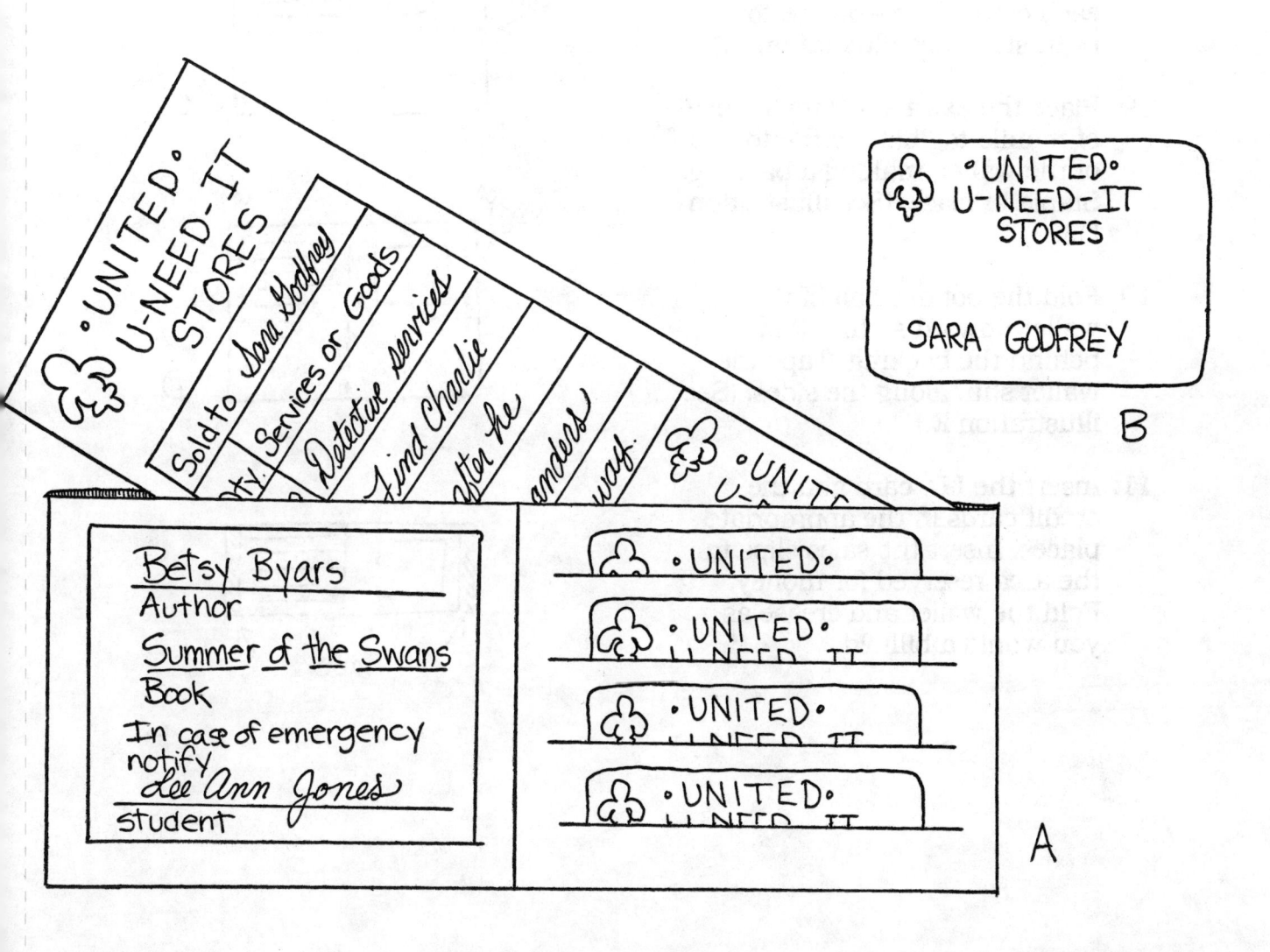

43

5. Decorate the credit cards appropriately. (See illustration B.) Print one character's name at the bottom of each card.

6. Make a sales slip 3½ x 7 inches for each character who owns a credit card. On each sales slip, describe a service or good(s) that the character needs in the story.

7. Make an I.D. card, 3¾ x 3¾ inches. In a space 3 x 3 inches on the card, write the author's name, the book title and the student's name.

8. Unfold the wallet. Cut a square, 3 x 3 inches, on the top left side. Make slits two-and-three-quarter inches long—one for each credit card—on the top right side. (See illustration C.)

9. Place the extra 4 x 8 inch piece of manila tag behind the top half of the wallet, making a backing. Staple in place. (See illustration D.)

10. Fold the bottom half of the wallet upward so that it is behind the backing. Tape the wallet shut along the sides. (See illustration E.)

11. Insert the I.D. card and the credit cards in the appropriate places. Insert the sales slips in the area reserved for money. Fold the wallet and crease as you would a billfold.

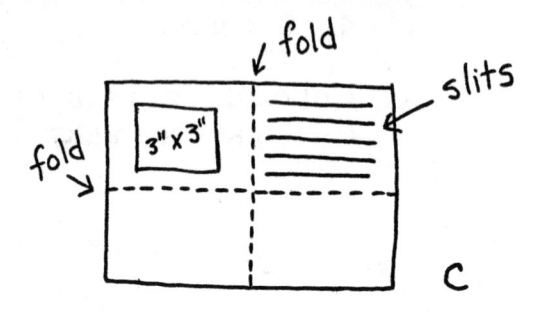

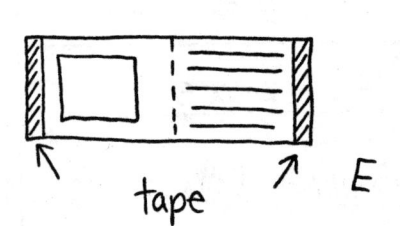

LOCKER ROOM

Use this "gym" of an idea to get ahead of the book report game for sports-related books.

1. Use a cigar or school box for the locker. Cover the top and sides with pieces of construction paper. Make locker markings with a black marker. (See illustration.)

2. Place three small plastic hooks with peel-and-stick backing on the inside of the locker.

3. Make symbols for the important characters or events in the book. Number each symbol.

4. On the back of the symbol, write its significance in the book.

5. Punch holes in the symbols and hang them on the hooks.

6. Draw the main character on the inside of the locker door. Write the name of the book and the author on a speech bubble.

HOE! HOE! HOE!

Characters in a book grow in many ways. This garden is planted with the attitudes, habits, friendships and feelings that are cultivated in your book.

1. Make a seed packet from a library pocket for each major character in the book.

2. Write the character's name on the front of the pocket. On the back of the pocket, write a statement about the character's personality.

3. Staple each pocket to a popsicle stick.

4. Use the flower pattern to make at least two flowers for each character.

5. On the front of the flower, write the habit, attitude, friendship or feeling that the character needs to cultivate.

6. On the back of the flower, explain why the character needs to cultivate the trait.

7. Staple the flowers to the popsicle sticks.

Lizzie lied to get attention and because she didn't like herself.

Honesty

Lizzie needs to cultivate honesty so that friends like Sara will like her. Her life would be less confused if she didn't have to remember all those lies.

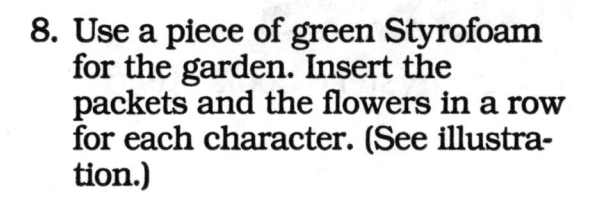

8. Use a piece of green Styrofoam for the garden. Insert the packets and the flowers in a row for each character. (See illustration.)

9. Use the pattern to make a scarecrow. Write the book title and the author on the moon. Mount the scarecrow on a popsicle stick.

10. Insert the scarecrow into the back of the garden.

STICKY FINGERS

This idea will go hand-in-glove with your mystery book. Keep the characters at your fingertips.

1. In order to make a "hand book," trace your hand on manila tagboard. Make one "hand" for each of the main characters in the book and two "hands" for the front and back covers.

2. Use a stamp pad to make a fingerprint on each character's hand. Decorate the fingerprint to match the description of the character in the book. (See illustration.)

3. Describe the character's role in the mystery next to the appropriate fingerprint.

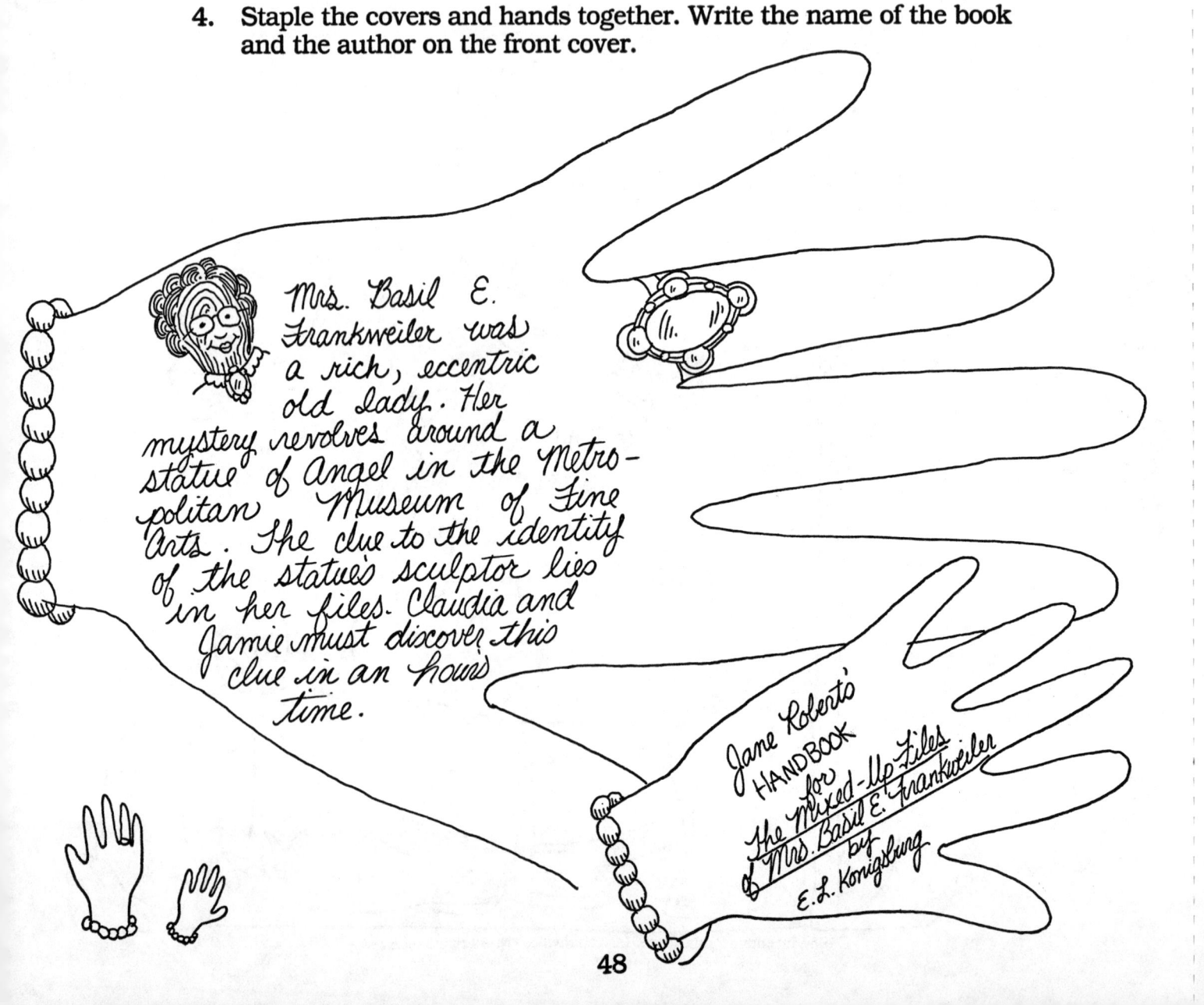

4. Staple the covers and hands together. Write the name of the book and the author on the front cover.

Mrs. Basil E. Frankweiler was a rich, eccentric old lady. Her mystery revolves around a statue of Angel in the Metropolitan Museum of Fine Arts. The clue to the identity of the statue's sculptor lies in her files. Claudia and Jamie must discover this clue in an hour's time.

Jane Robert's HANDBOOK for The Mixed-Up Files of Mrs. Basil E. Frankweiler by E. L. Konigsburg

OUT OF THIS WORLD

Once in a blue moon, your kids will need to blast off with science fiction. Send them into orbit with this idea!

1. Use a potato chip or tennis ball can for the body of the rocket ship. Cover the can with paper or foil and decorate appropriately. Write the name and the author of the book on the side of the can.

2. Decorate a set of old-fashioned clothespins to resemble the characters in your book. Use felt, markers, tempera or construction paper for clothing and features. Label each character by name.

3. Pretend you are one of the main characters in the book (perhaps the ship's captain). Make a tape of the most dramatic event(s) in the book.

4. Place the tape and the characters into the can.

5. Use half of a panty hose egg as the nose cone of the rocket. Place the egg on top of the can.

JUST HATCHED!

You can put all your eggs in one basket with this project that won't leave you with egg on your face at book reporting time!

1. Use the chicken patterns to make a front and back from tagboard and decorate. Fold the back pattern piece along the dotted line. Cut to the dotted line at the top edge of the back pattern piece. (See illustration A.)

2. Match points A and B on the pattern front to points A and B on the pattern back, respectively. Glue the folded flap of the back piece to the back side of the front piece.

3. Draw an eye and a beak on the back side of the chicken.

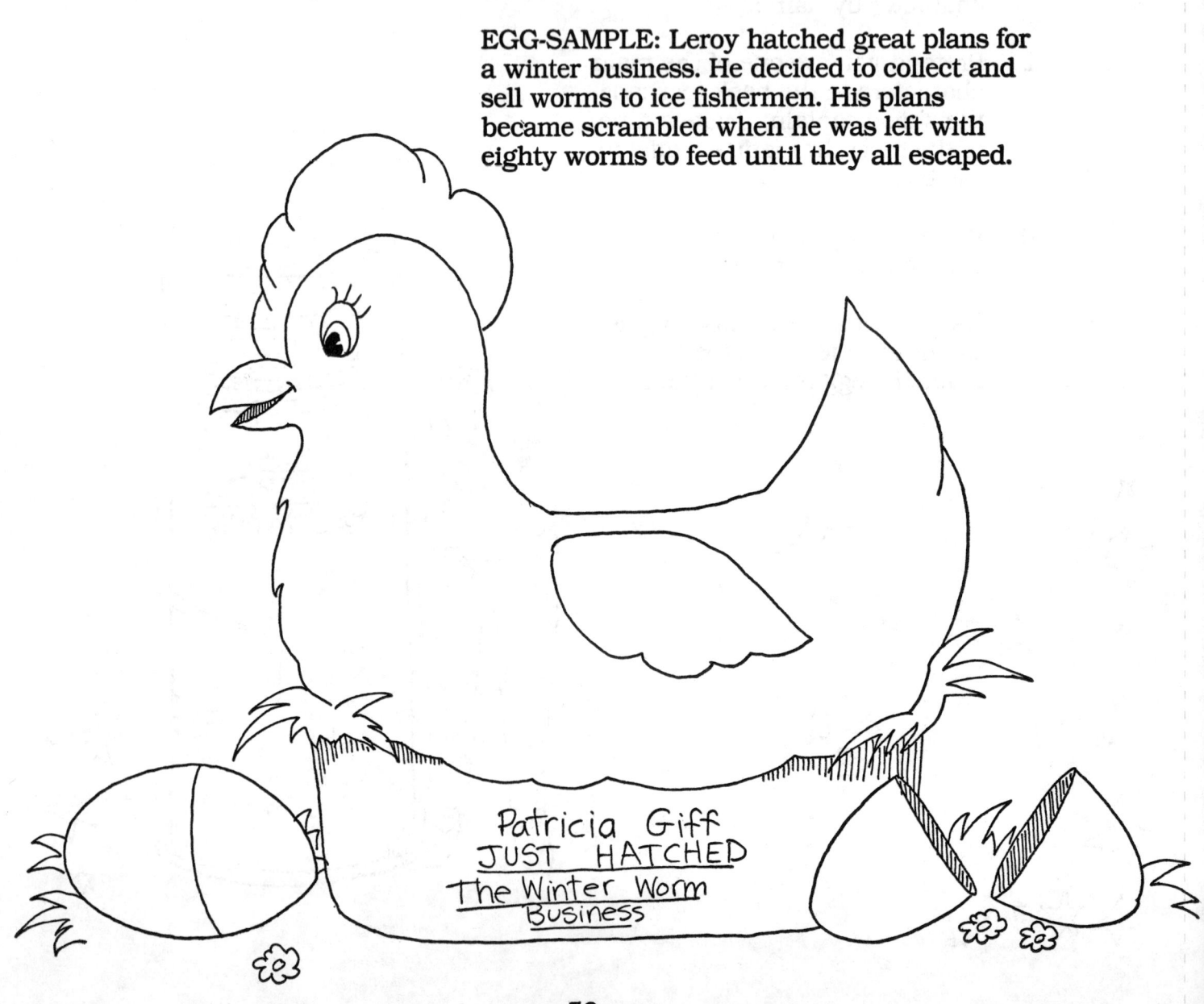

EGG-SAMPLE: Leroy hatched great plans for a winter business. He decided to collect and sell worms to ice fishermen. His plans became scrambled when he was left with eighty worms to feed until they all escaped.

4. Use an 8-ounce whipped topping container for the nest. Write the book title and the author on one side of the nest. (See illustration.)

5. Use one small colored plastic egg for each main character. Use a long strip of paper to tell how the character:

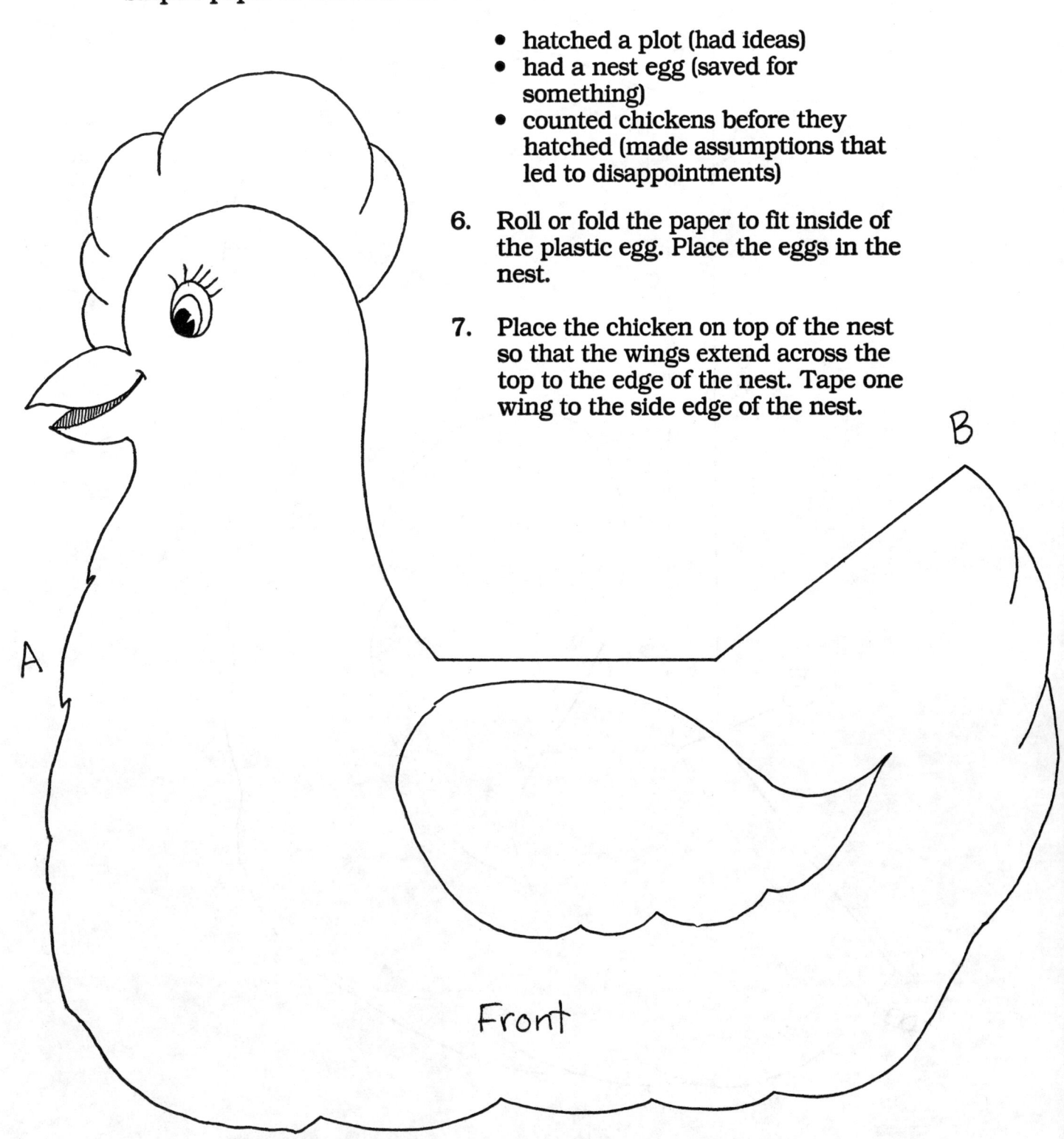

   - hatched a plot (had ideas)
   - had a nest egg (saved for something)
   - counted chickens before they hatched (made assumptions that led to disappointments)

6. Roll or fold the paper to fit inside of the plastic egg. Place the eggs in the nest.

7. Place the chicken on top of the nest so that the wings extend across the top to the edge of the nest. Tape one wing to the side edge of the nest.

Front

©1984 Incentive Publications, Inc., Nashville, TN. All rights reserved.

A

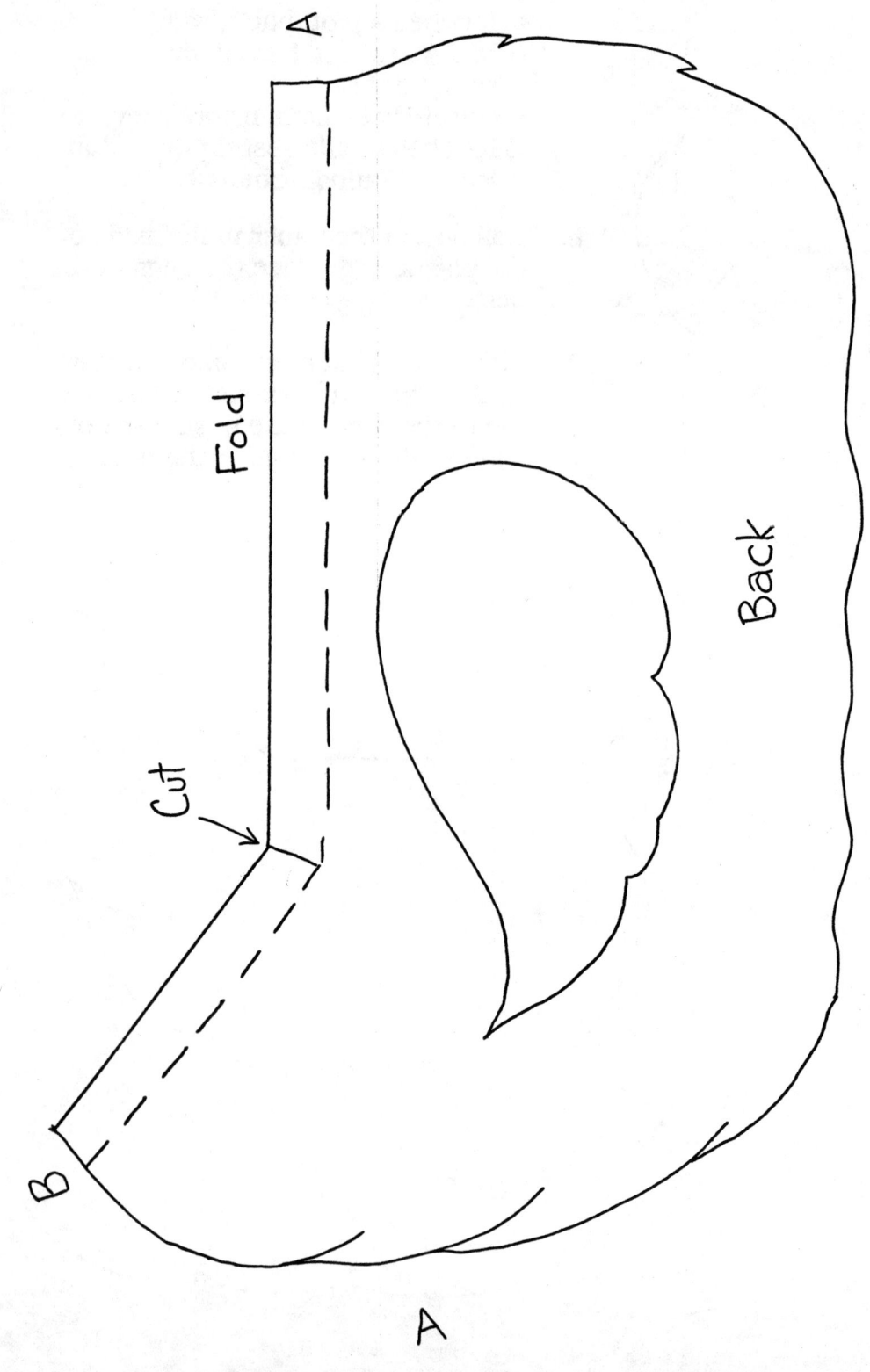

Fold

Cut

B

Back

A

SHOOT FOR THE STARS

Skyrocket to fame with this dynamite project for characters with lofty ambitions!

1. Make a firecracker for each important character in the book. Use a bathroom tissue tube for the firecracker.

2. Make a circle from posterboard or cardboard the same diameter as the tube. Punch a hole in the center of the circle. Insert a pipe cleaner into the hole as a fuse. Place the circle and the fuse in one end of the tube. See illustration.

3. Cover the tube with white paper. Decorate the lower half of the tube to resemble a firecracker. On the upper half of the firecracker, explain how a character reached a goal or satisfied an ambition.

4. To make the skyrocket, use another tissue tube. Cover the tube with white paper and decorate appropriately. Make a cone from tagboard or construction paper. Write the book title and the author on the cone. Attach the cone to one end of the tube.

5. Make streamers from strips of colored paper or ribbon. Attach one end of the streamers halfway up the inside of the tube.

6. Use an aluminum pie pan for the mobile. Punch a hole in the center of the pan. Thread string, yarn or ribbon through the hole. Knot the string on both the top and bottom sides of the pan, leaving the string hanging above and below the pan.

7. Make evenly spaced holes around the edge of the pan. Thread string through each of the holes. Knot each string on the top of the mobile to secure it in place.

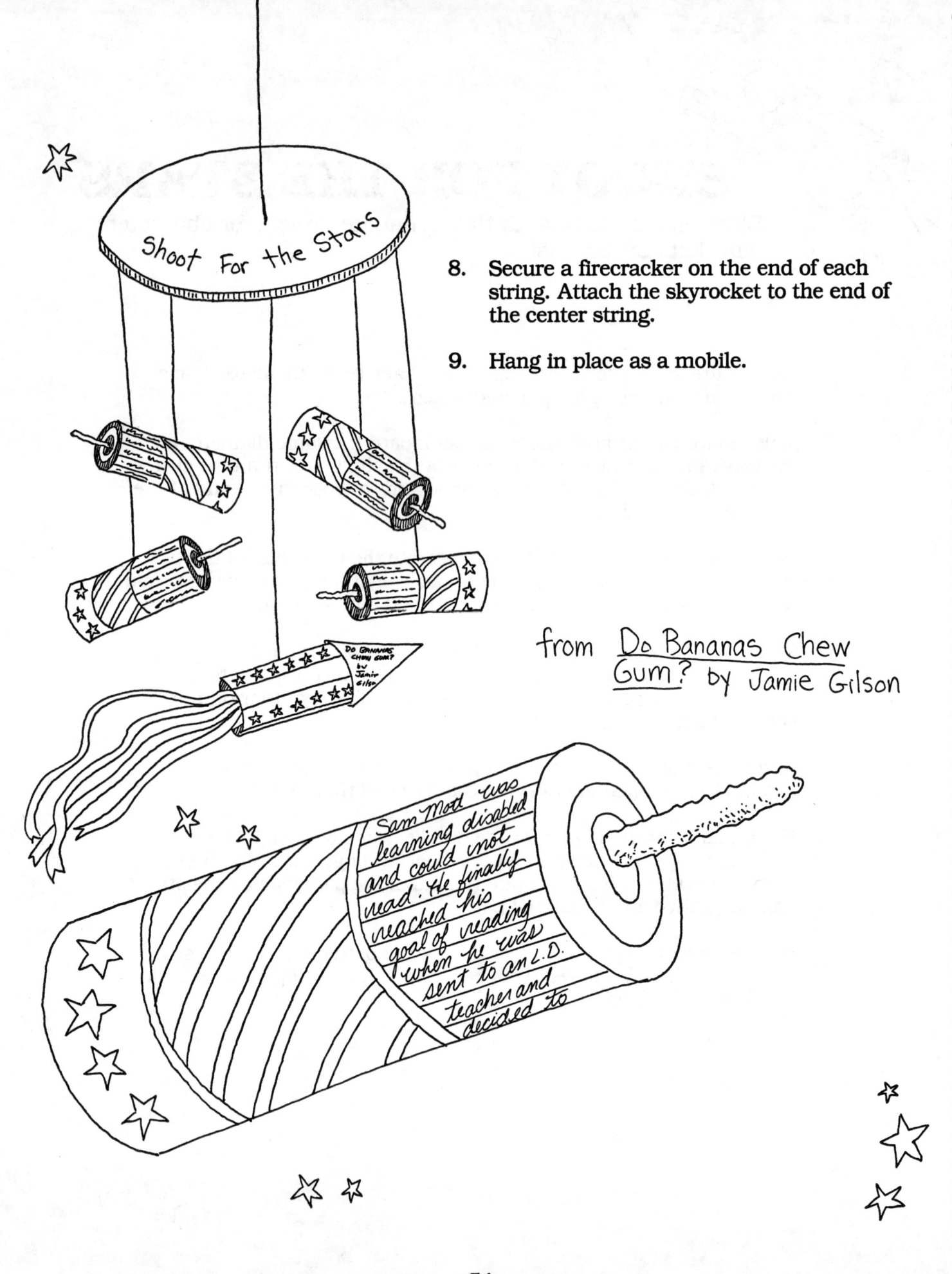

8. Secure a firecracker on the end of each string. Attach the skyrocket to the end of the center string.

9. Hang in place as a mobile.

from *Do Bananas Chew Gum?* by Jamie Gilson

54

COLOR GUARD

Add a little color to your book reporting! Make giant crayons for characters who guard their feelings.

1. Make a crayon for each important character in your book using the crayon pattern. Choose a color for the character that is significant in that character's life.

2. In the large oval, write a brief explanation of the significance of the color to the character. You may want to show how and when characters:

   - were red with anger
   - felt blue
   - had a yellow streak
   - felt green with envy
   - flew into a purple rage
   - were good as gold
   - turned white as a ghost
   - were in a black mood
   - made brownie points
   - were tickled pink
   - were born with a silver spoon in their mouths

3. Decorate the small oval to resemble the face of the character. Label each crayon with the character's name. (See illustration.)

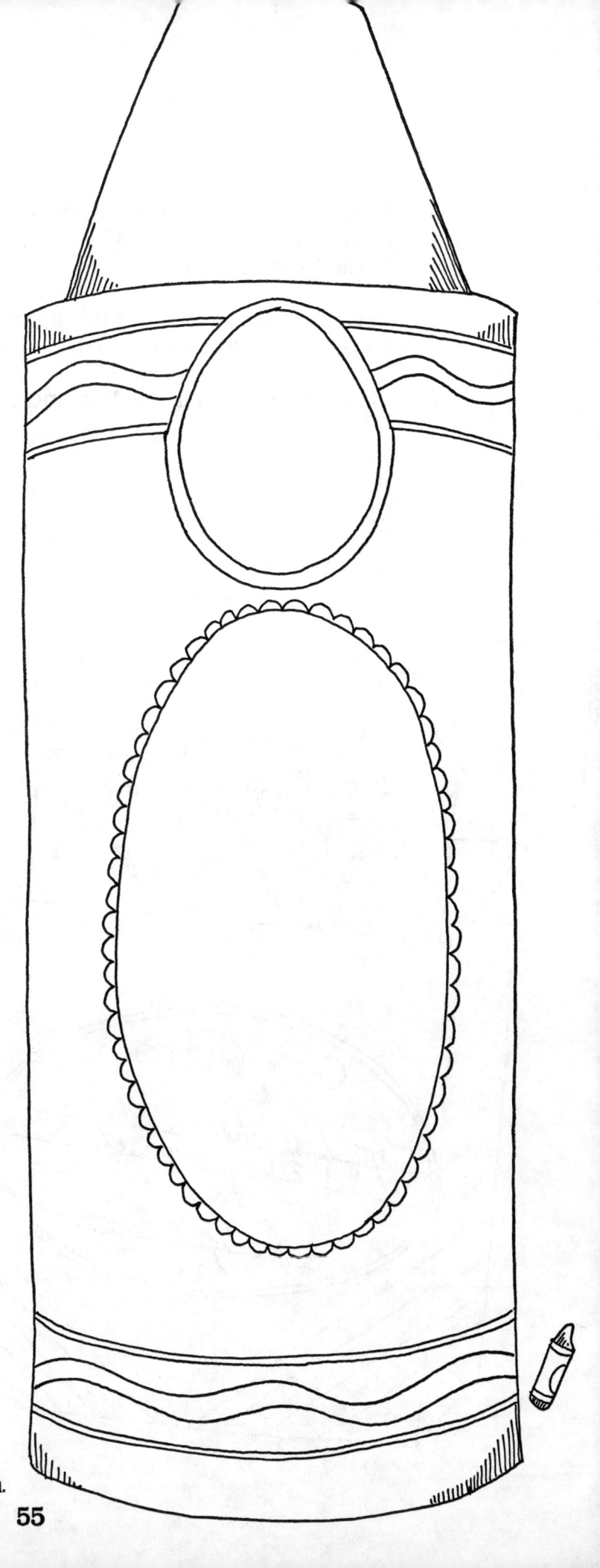

©1984 Incentive Publications, Inc., Nashville, TN. All rights reserved.

4. Make a box for the crayons from a large detergent box. Cut each side of the box front at an angle. (See illustration.) Leave the lid attached to the back of the box.

5. Decorate the box to resemble a crayon box. Write the name of the book and the author on a label. Glue the label on the front of the box.

6. Place the crayons in the box and display.

CROSS SECTION

Up a tree about your next book project? Don't be stumped! Use this idea to show how the characters have grown.

1. Use cans to make stumps for each main character in your book. The largest can should be used for the most important character, the second largest can for the next most important character, and so on. All the cans should be able to nest.

2. Cover the cans with wood-grained adhesive paper. The open end of the cans will become the bottoms of the tree stumps.

3. Make the tops of the stumps from circles of tan construction paper. Draw growth rings on each one.

4. On each growth ring, tell how the character has shown growth in personality, ideas, emotions and abilities. Circles may also be used to tell how a character has outgrown people, places, things and ideas.

5. Glue the circles on the tops of the appropriate cans.

6. Make leaves from green construction paper. Write the book title and the author on the leaves. Glue the leaves to the front of the largest can.

7. Place the cans inside each other, from smallest to largest.

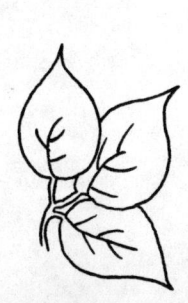

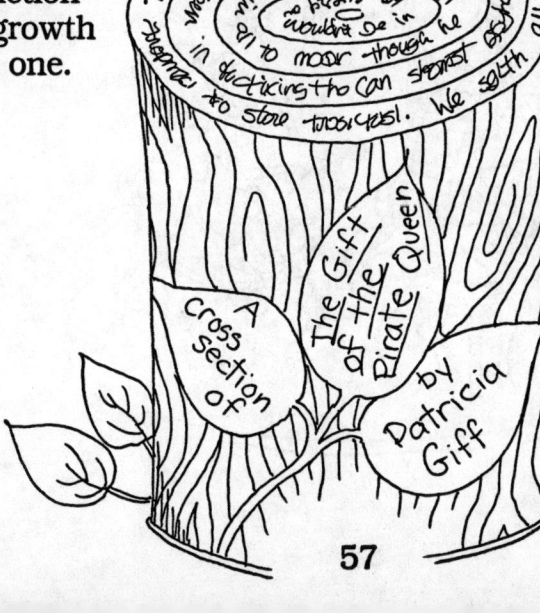

HOLD YOUR HORSES

Sometimes the characters in your book lead you on a merry chase. Use your horse sense and make a carousel to show their "ups and downs."

1. Make a carousel horse and rider for each main character in your book using the pattern. Decorate each rider as a character. Write the character's name on the dotted line of the saddle blanket. Cut out each horse and rider and fold on the dotted line.

2. Use popsicle sticks for the carousel poles. Place these sticks between the front and back of the horse and rider. Glue or tape the stick in place. Staple or glue the front and back of the horse and rider together.

3. Use the pattern to make a flag for each horse and rider. Write the "ups and downs" (problems and solutions, good times and bad, etc.) of the character on the flag. Mount the flag on a toothpick as you mounted the horse and rider.

4. Use two round pieces of Styrofoam for the base and top of the carousel. Each piece should be at least twelve inches in diameter.

58

5. Cover a tall potato chip can with decorative paper. Press the can into the center of one piece of Styrofoam. Arrange the horses and riders one-and-one-half inches from the edge of the base. Press these sticks into the Styrofoam. (See illustration.)

6. Press the center of the second piece of Styrofoam into the top of the can. This makes the carousel top.

7. Place each flag over the character it describes. Press each toothpick into the Styrofoam.

8. Make one flag for the top center of the carousel. Write the book title and author on this flag. Mount the flag on a popsicle stick and press into the center top of the carousel.

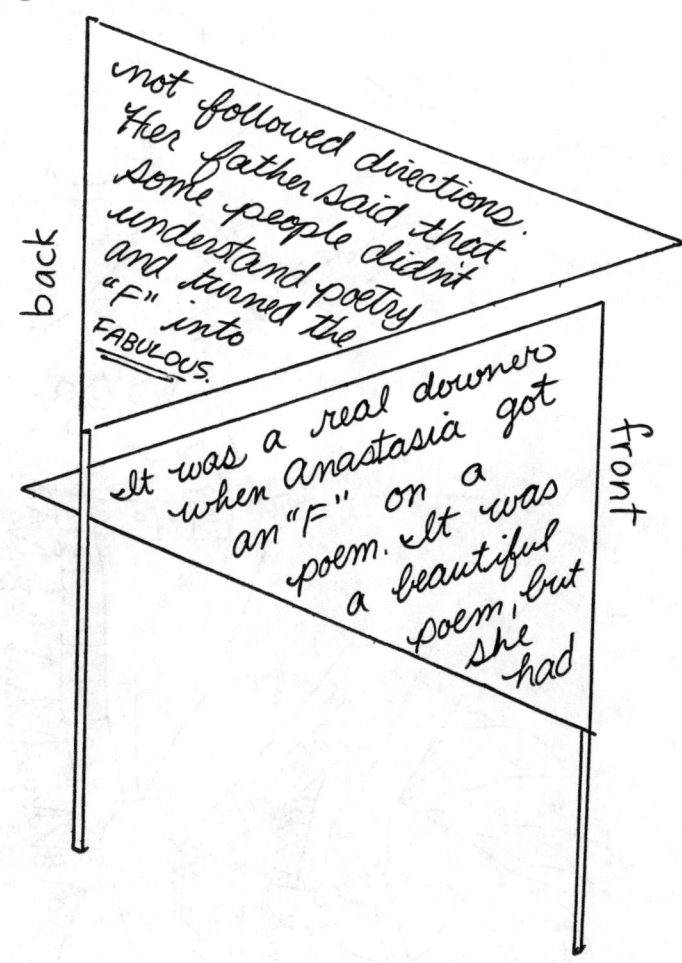

←fold→

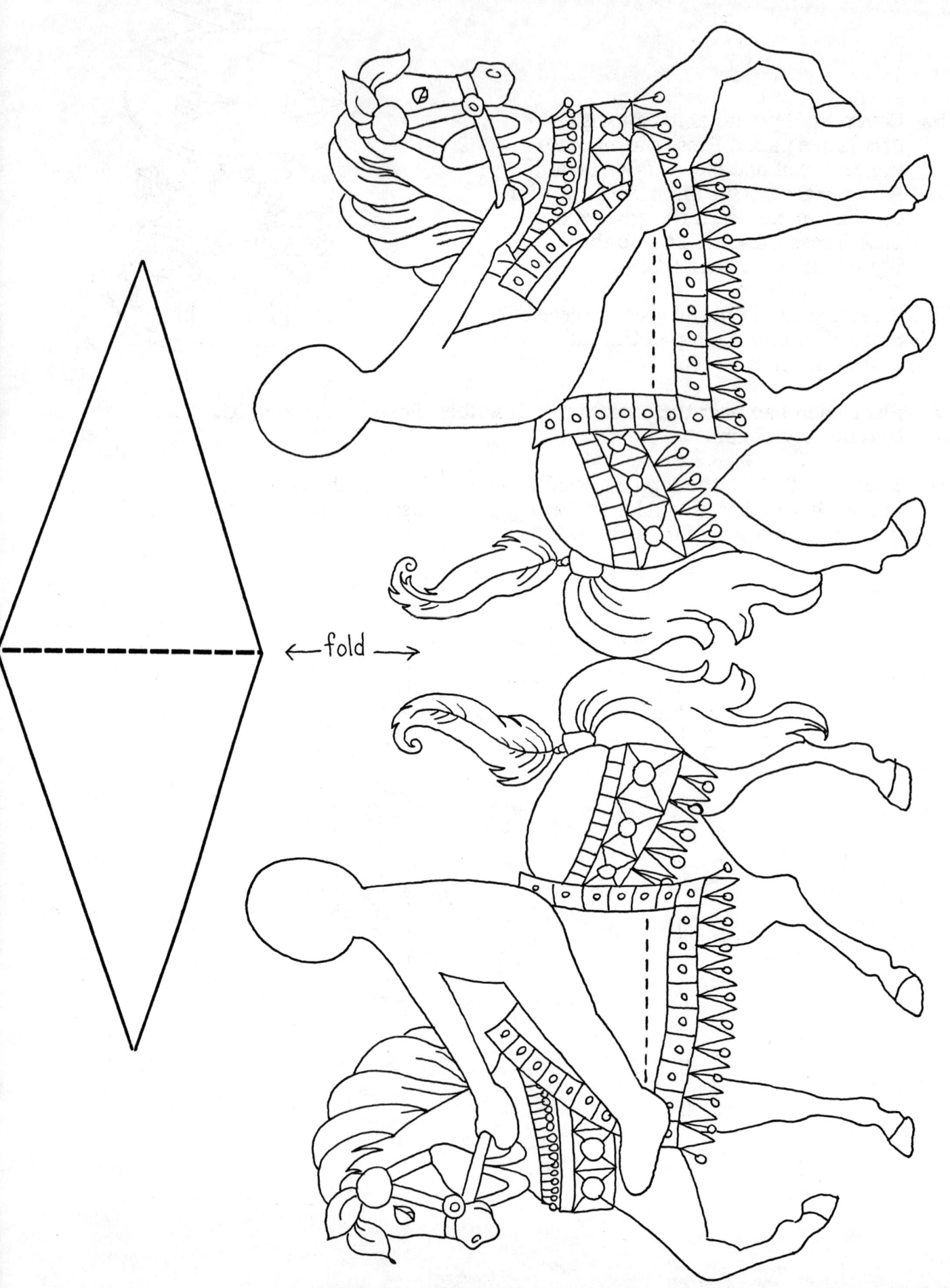

©1984 Incentive Publications, Inc., Nashville, TN. All rights reserved.

60

PARTY LINE

Don't get your wires crossed over book projects! This idea could be the talk of the town when you show how characters gossip.

1. Use the pattern to make a telephone base out of posterboard. Write the book title and the author on the dial. Punch a hole in the top of the base at the dot.

2. Make the telephone receivers from a long piece of kraft paper. Fold the paper back and forth, making sure each fold of paper measures seven-and-one-quarter inches long. Place the dotted edge of the receiver on the right fold of the top piece. Trace the receiver. Cut out the receivers as you would paper dolls. Leave the folded edge uncut. A connected length of receivers should be the result.

3. Punch a hole in the receivers at the dot.

4. On each receiver, explain how the book character(s) gossiped or could have been the subject of gossip.

5. Place a brad through the hole in the telephone base with the prongs facing you. Place the brad through the holes in the folded receivers to display.

©1984 Incentive Publications, Inc., Nashville, TN. All rights reserved.

RAIN OR SHINE

All wet when it's book project time? If it's raining on your parade, use these umbrellas to tell how characters overcame their rainy days!

1. Use a 14-ounce frozen juice can for the umbrella stand. Cover it with solid colored paper and decorate.

2. Make a "puddle" of blue paper. Write the book title and the author on the puddle. Glue the puddle to the bottom of the can. (See illustration.)

3. Use brightly colored posterboard or tagboard for umbrellas. Make an umbrella for each character who experienced problems, had fair weather friends, needed to save for a rainy day or needed sheltering.

4. Write the character's name on the handle of the umbrella. On the lines of the umbrella, explain the character's situation.

5. Place the umbrellas in the umbrella stand.

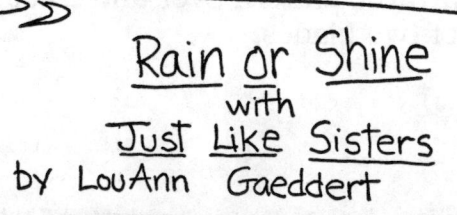

Rain or Shine with *Just Like Sisters* by LouAnn Gaeddert

FAN-TASTIC!

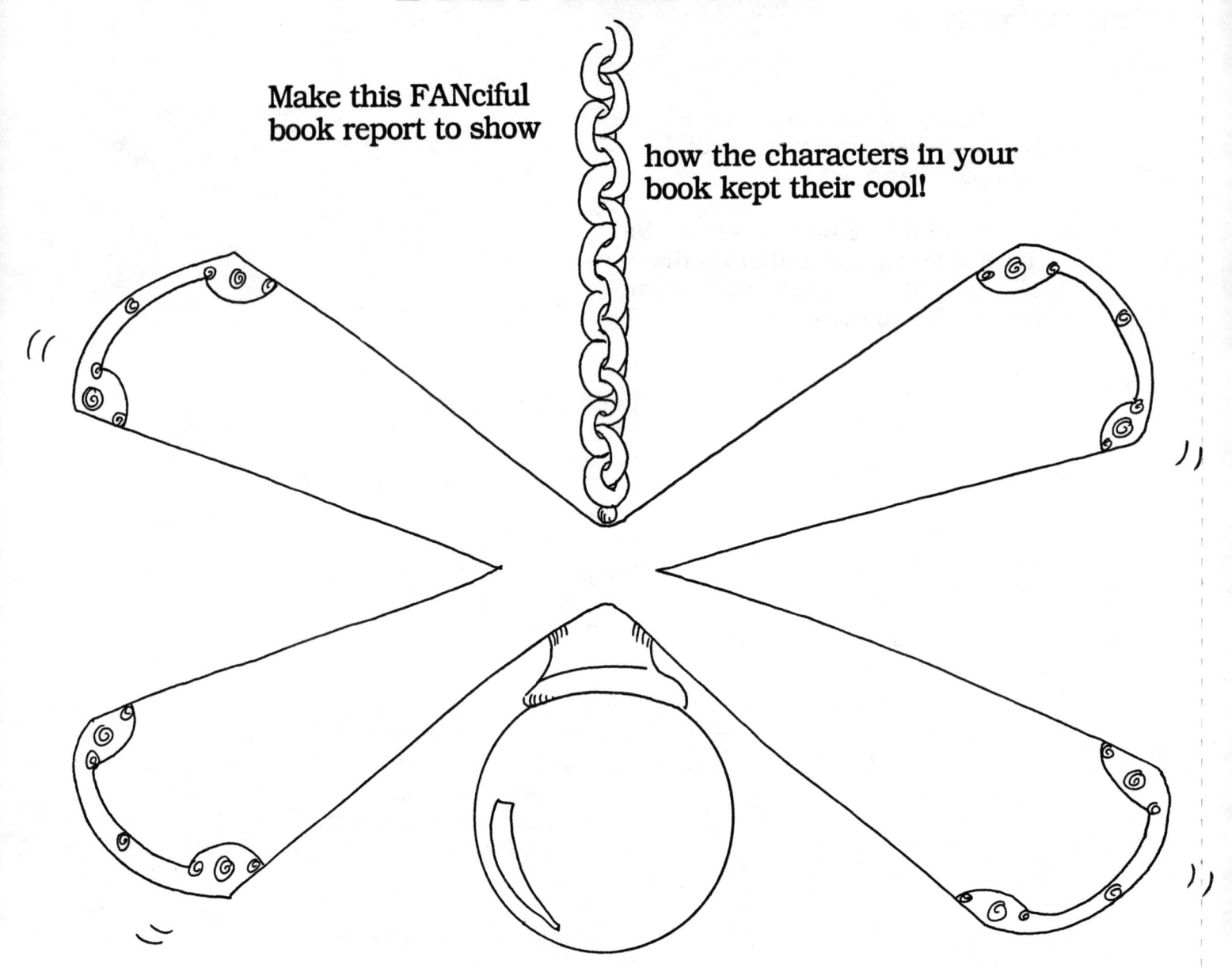

Make this FANciful book report to show how the characters in your book kept their cool!

1. Use an overhead projector to enlarge the fan blade pattern to the desired size. Use a piece of posterboard or tagboard twice as long as the desired size for one blade. The dotted line on the pattern should be placed in the middle of the posterboard or tagboard. After tracing one blade, turn the pattern over and trace the opposite blade. Make another set of two blades.

©1984 Incentive Publications, Inc., Nashville, TN. All rights reserved.

2. Punch two holes in each blade at the "Xs."

3. Make a light fixture from tagboard or posterboard. Punch one hole in the top of the fixture at the "X."

4. Make a chain from ¾-inch strips of tagboard. Secure each strip with staples.

5. Write the book title and the author on the light fixture.

6. On the underside of each blade, write the name of a main character. Tell how that character kept his or her cool in the story.

7. Loop yarn, string or ribbon through the holes you have punched.

8. Secure the blades and the fixture to the chain with the yarn. Hang as a mobile.

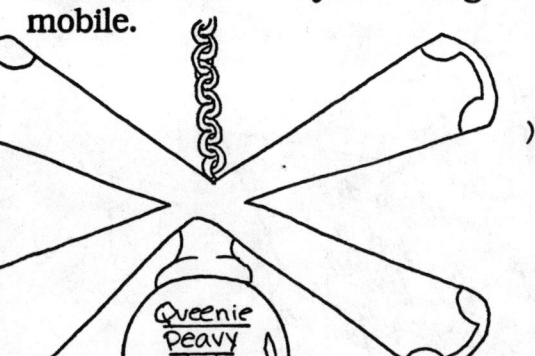

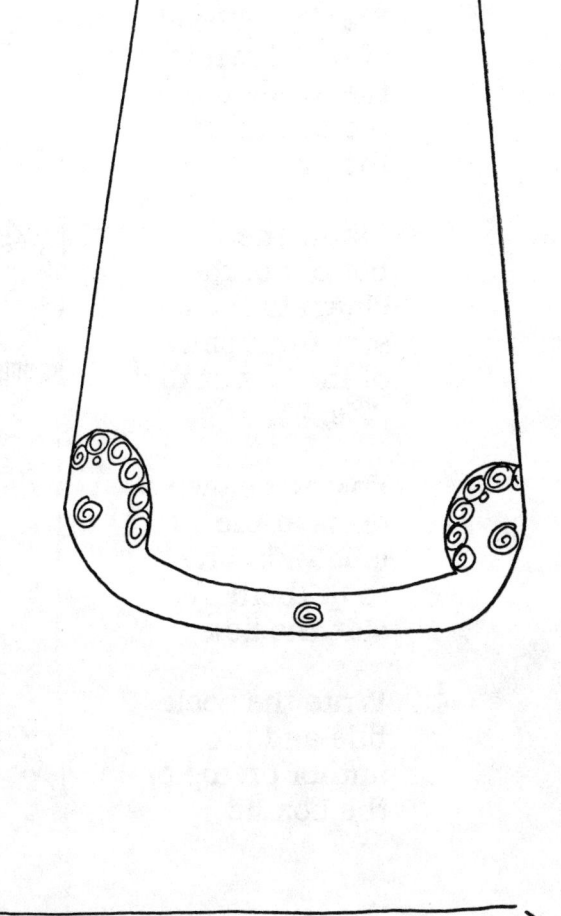

©1984 Incentive Publications, Inc., Nashville, TN. All rights reserved.

JUMP TO A CONCLUSION

Need a poppin' good idea for a book project? This one will help your readers spring into action with characters who jumped to conclusions.

1. Use manila paper to make the clown. Decorate appropriately.

2. Use a box measuring approximately 4½ x 6 x 2½ inches. Remove the two side flaps from under the top lid. Cover the box and lid with adhesive paper.

3. Staple the head of the clown to the inside top of the box lid at the "X."

   Staple the bottom of the clown to the inside front panel of the box at the "Xs."

   Fold the clown's arms at the elbows in order to fit them inside the box.

4. Write the book title and the author on top of the box lid.

from <u>Wish, Come True</u> by Mary Q. Steele

Meg jumped to the conclusion that the ring she found was magic. She also jumped to the conclusion that Aunt Louise was a dull woman who was not interested in magic.

5. Make star shapes for the main characters in the book. Write a character's name on a star and tell how that character jumped to a conclusion. If necessary, use more than one star for each character. Glue each character's star(s) on a different side of the box.

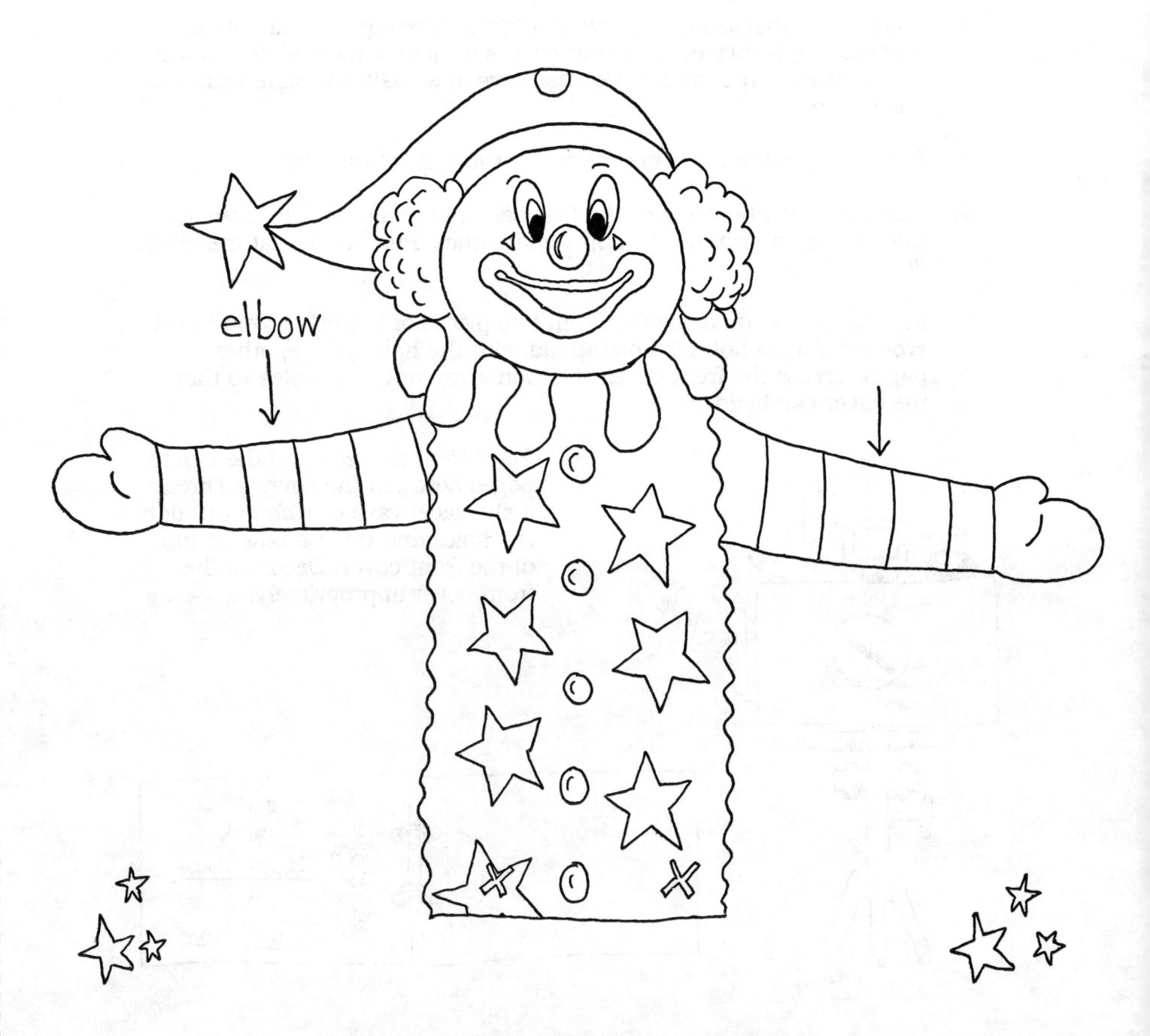

elbow

©1984 INCENTIVE PUBLICATIONS, Inc., Nashville, TN. All rights reserved.

GET THE PICTURE?

Picture this idea for a book project idea! A family album will portray your students as winners.

1. Duplicate one snapshot page from tagboard for each major character in your book.

2. Use photos, magazine pictures or original drawings to illustrate important people, places, things or events in the characters' lives. Place the pictures in the frames. Use the lines to explain the significance of the pictures.

3. Punch two holes at the black dots on the edge of the page.

4. Duplicate the title page for the first page of the album. Write the book title and the author on the appropriate lines. Punch holes at the black dots.

5. Make a front and back cover from two pieces of brightly colored posterboard. Punch holes to correspond with the holes on the other pages. Crease the front cover one inch away from the holes so that the cover can bend.

6. Place the title page and the album pages between the covers. Thread a shoelace, yarn or ribbon through the holes and tie in a bow on top of the front cover. Decorate the front cover appropriately.

's Snapshots

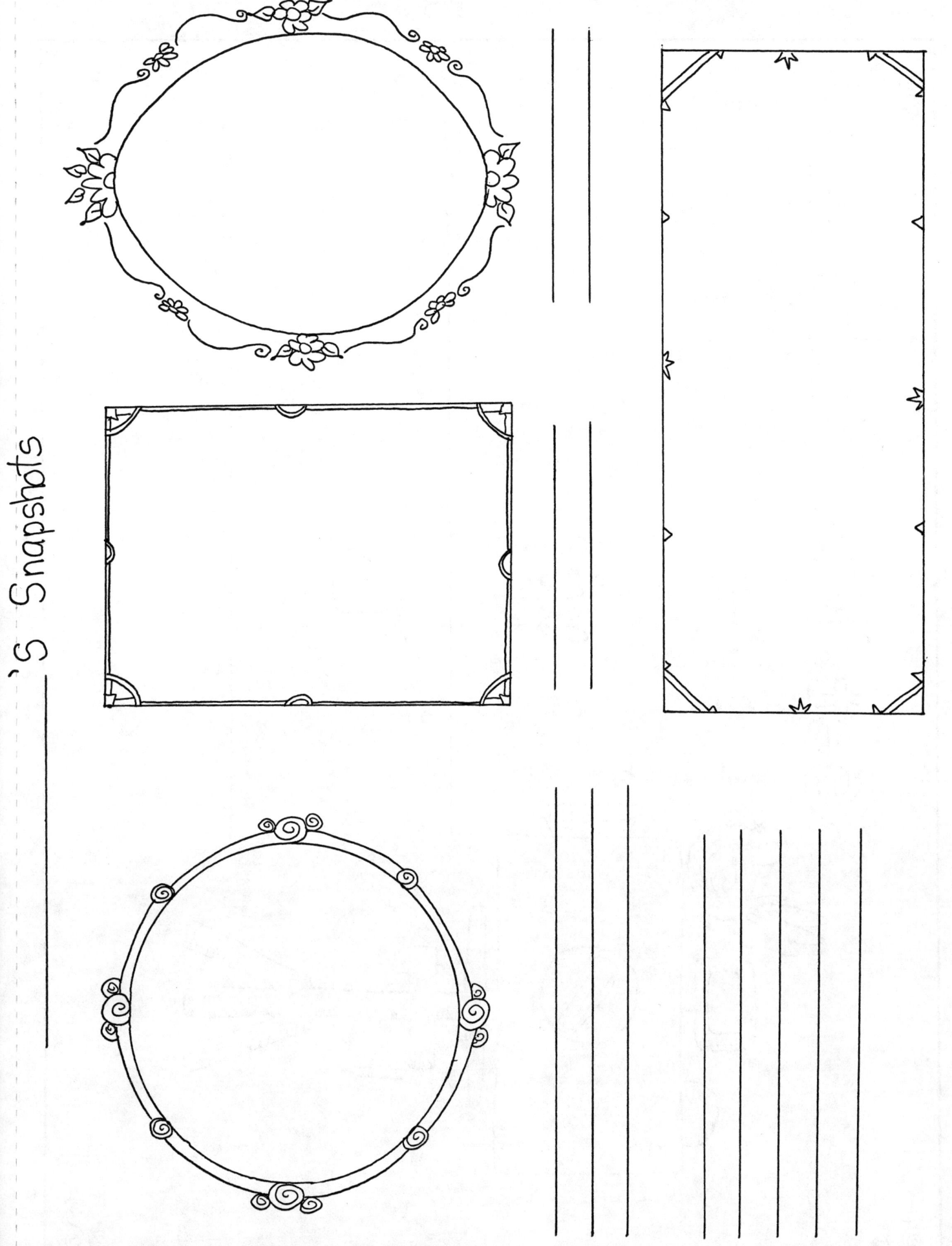

©1984 Incentive Publications, Inc., Nashville, TN. All rights reserved.

Get The Picture?

with _____

by _____

"click"

©1984 Incentive Publications, Inc., Nashville, TN. All rights reserved.

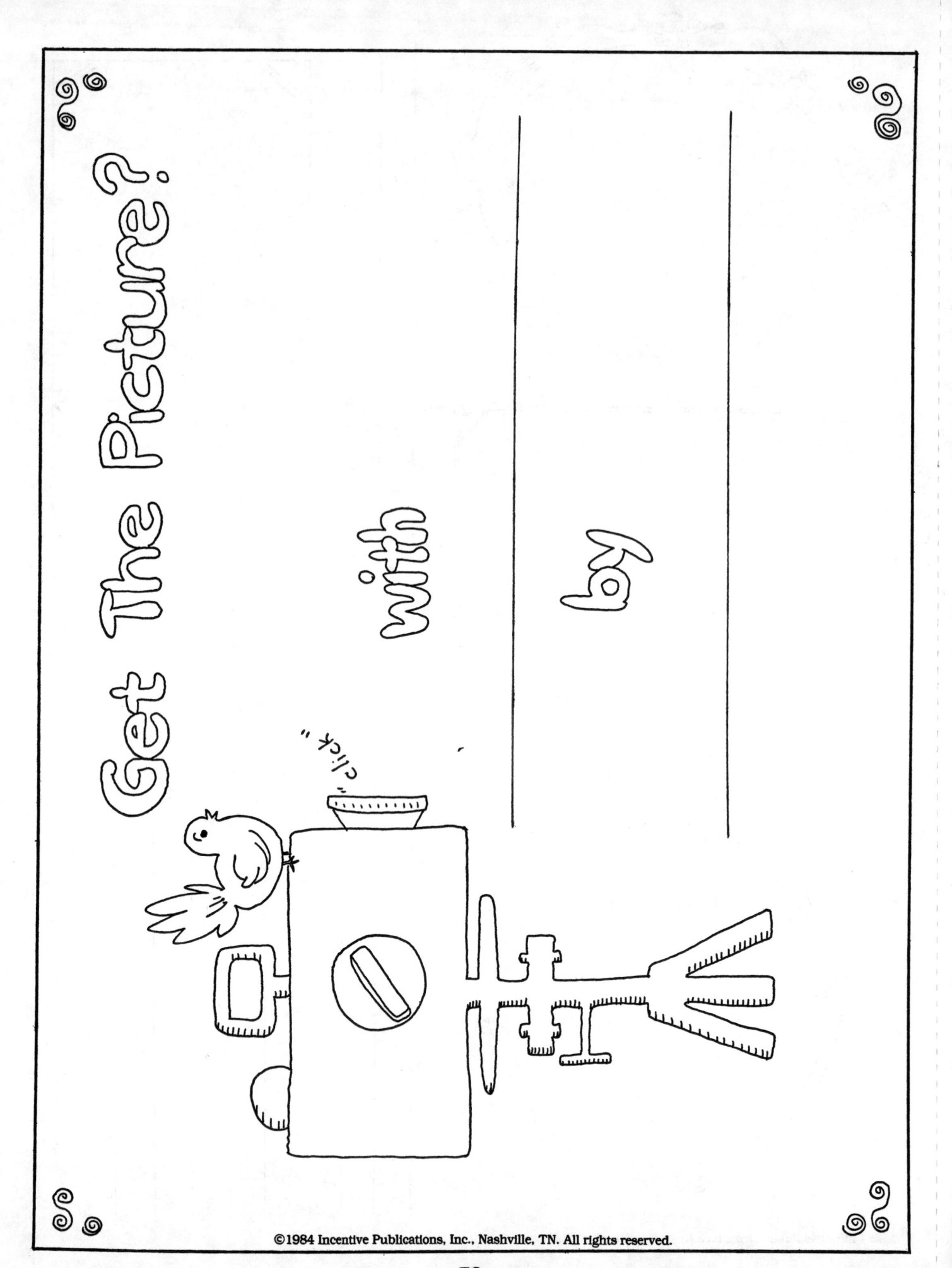

70

PRESERVE IT!

Are your students in a jam when it comes to book reporting? Get them out of that sticky situation with this sweet idea!

1. Use a jelly or canning jar for each main character in the book.

2. Write the character's name on a label. Attach the label to the top of the jar.

3. Use a different "flavor" of jam (paper) for each jar (purple for grape, red for cherry, yellow for pear, etc.). Tell how that character kept, preserved or maintained something (an idea, object or feeling) in the book.

4. Roll the paper and place it in the jar so that the writing can be read from the outside of the jar.

5. Use a basket or a shoe box as a container for the jars.

6. Label the basket with the book title and the author.

from *Sounder* by William H. Armstrong

The Boy — The boy kept track of his father during his imprisonment.

Mother — Mother kept the family together and preserved a sense of security.

Father — Father maintained his faith that he would one day return home.

Sounder — Sounder kept a vigil for his master who was in jail.

STRUT YOUR STUFF

You can point with pride to a project that will be a feather in your cap.

1. Use a small margarine tub to make the middle section of the peacock. Cut a circle of fabric ten inches in diameter. Run a basting thread one-half inch in along the edge of the fabric. Place the margarine tub in the center of the fabric, small side down. Draw the basting thread tight, gathering the fabric around the tub. Baste again around the circle, using the original basting thread as a guide. Knot the thread and cut.

2. Use the pattern to make the peacock head from tagboard. Write the book title and the author on the feathered lines of the peacock's body.

3. Use the pattern to make the peacock's tail from brightly colored tagboard. Use the feather lines on the tail to explain how one or more characters from the book displayed pride, or had something to be proud of.

4. Staple the peacock's head to the small side of the fabric-covered tub. Use the dotted lines on the tail as a guide for stapling on the tail to the large side of the tub where the gathering stitches are. Punch a hole in the top center "eye" of the tail and hang.

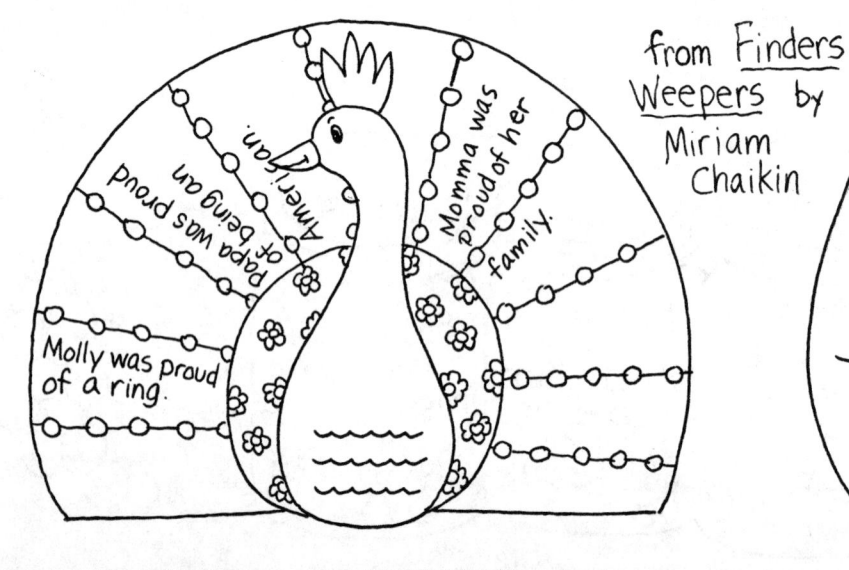

from *Finders Weepers* by Miriam Chaikin

©1984 Incentive Publications, Inc., Nashville, TN. All rights reserved.

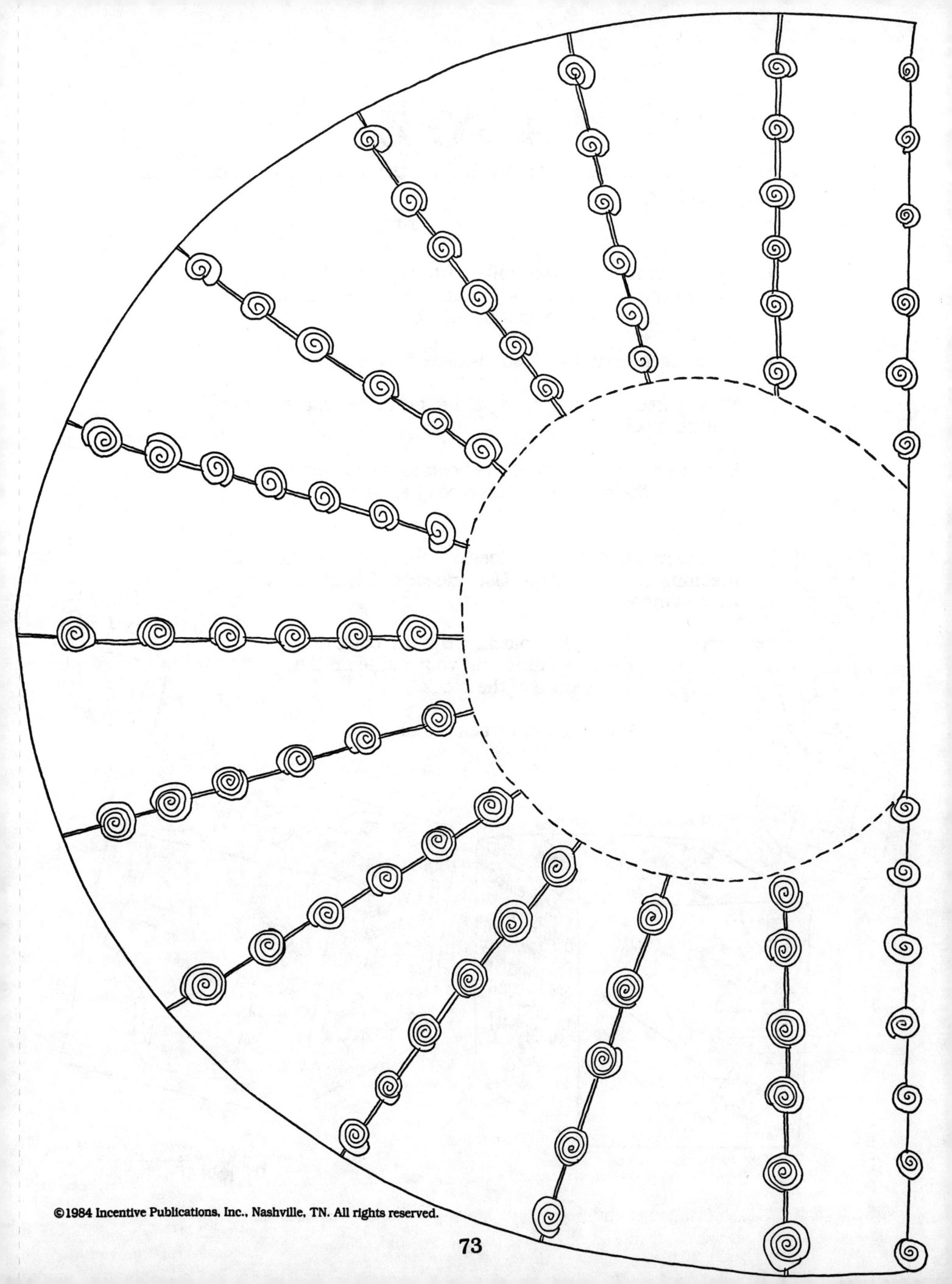

©1984 Incentive Publications, Inc., Nashville, TN. All rights reserved.

A TO Z

If your book reporting seems blocked up, try this project which is letter perfect!

1. Use ten individual-sized milk cartons for the blocks. Flatten the top of each carton and tape it together. The cartons should be flat on all sides.

2. Cover each carton with solid-colored paper.

3. Write three letters of the alphabet on three separate sides of each block.

4. Decide on a symbol from the book for each alphabet letter. Draw the symbol on the block beside the appropriate letter.

5. On the remaining blank sides of each block, explain the meaning of the symbols. Use one side of each block for each symbol.

6. On the last block, write the book title, author's name and your name on the blank sides of the block.

7. Make random stacks to display.

Ben invented a kite mobile for Amos. Ben used this kite to discover electricity.

Amos was the mouse who lived in Ben's hat. He took credit for all of Ben's inventions.

from *Ben and Me* by Robert Lawson

MASQUERADE

Go where the action is! Let your students speak up and wear the masks of the main character in this oral book reporting idea.

1. Often a character displays many feelings, pretends to be many things, works at different jobs, hides many emotions or wants to be something or someone he or she is not. Use the pattern to make masks from posterboard for the one main character in your book. Make one mask for each personality trait or emotion that the character displays. Decorate the masks appropriately.

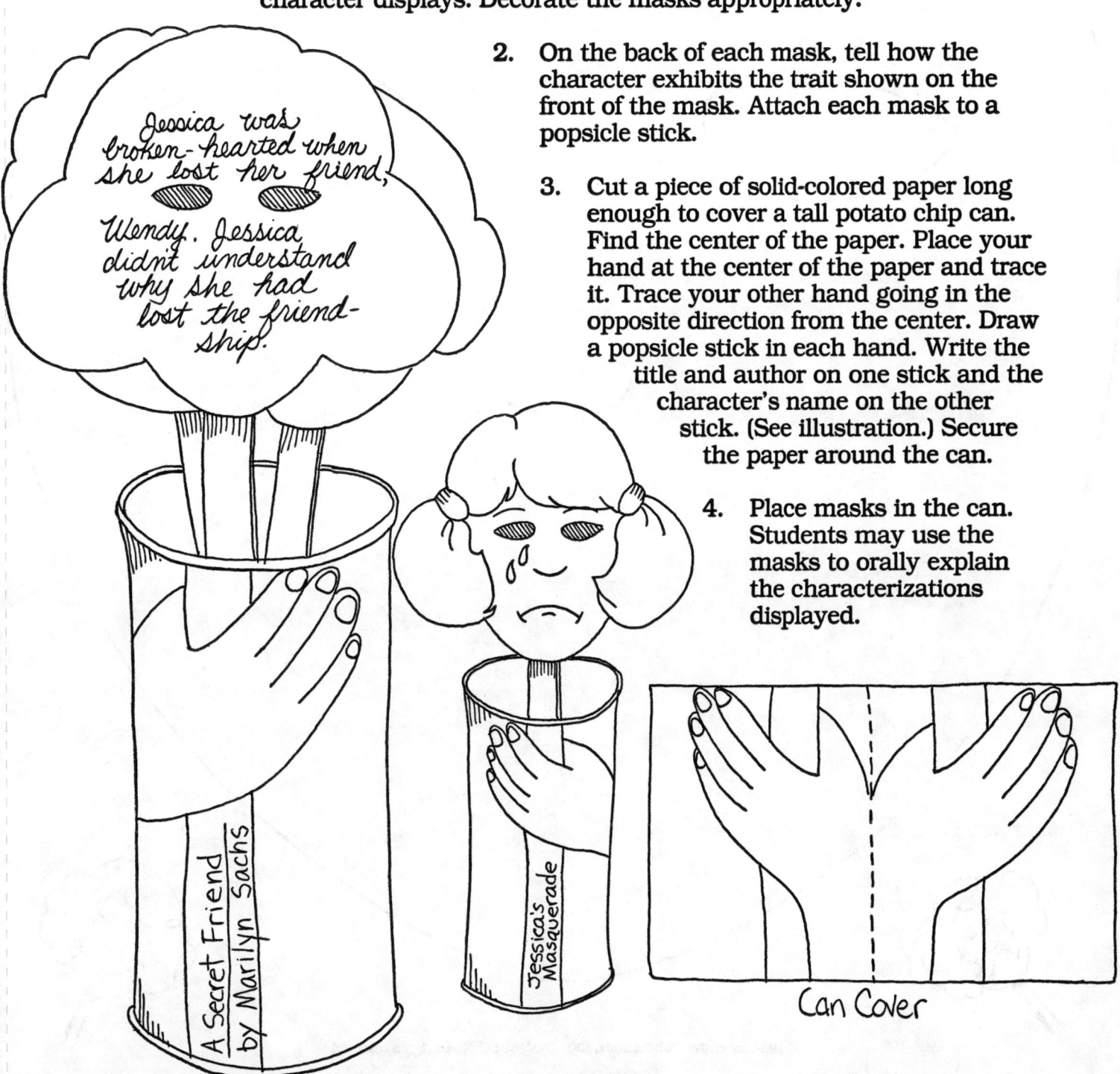

2. On the back of each mask, tell how the character exhibits the trait shown on the front of the mask. Attach each mask to a popsicle stick.

3. Cut a piece of solid-colored paper long enough to cover a tall potato chip can. Find the center of the paper. Place your hand at the center of the paper and trace it. Trace your other hand going in the opposite direction from the center. Draw a popsicle stick in each hand. Write the title and author on one stick and the character's name on the other stick. (See illustration.) Secure the paper around the can.

4. Place masks in the can. Students may use the masks to orally explain the characterizations displayed.

©1984 Incentive Publications, Inc., Nashville, TN. All rights reserved.

WEIGH YOUR WORDS

Is the weight of the world on your shoulders when it comes to book reports? On a scale of one to ten, this one's an ELEVEN!

1. Use the patterns on the following pages to make the scale from brightly colored tagboard or paper.

2. Cut out the pattern on page 80 along the inside of the dotted line AB. Cut out the remainder of the pattern along the outside of the dark line. Do the same with the pattern on page 79. Assemble the scale by matching points A and B and gluing in place. (See illustration.)

3. Write the book title and the author on the lines in the center of the scale.

4. Use the pattern to make an arrow from light-weight plastic. Attach the arrow to the scale's gauge at the dot. Use a brad.

5. On the outlined right foot, tell what the main character gained (objects, feelings, time, people, maturity, etc.). On the outlined left foot, explain what that same character lost.

6. Cover a large detergent box with adhesive paper. Glue the scales to the top of the box.

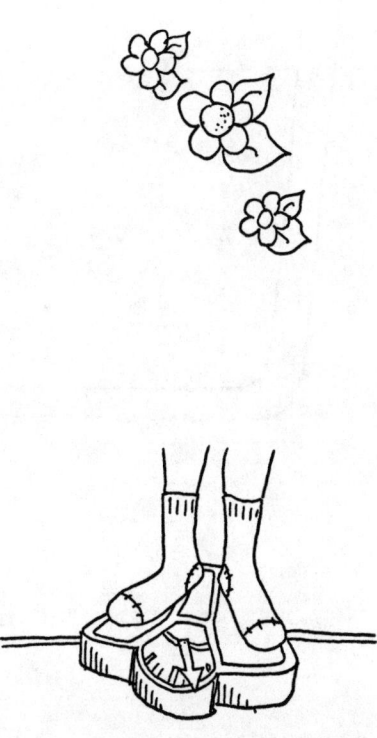

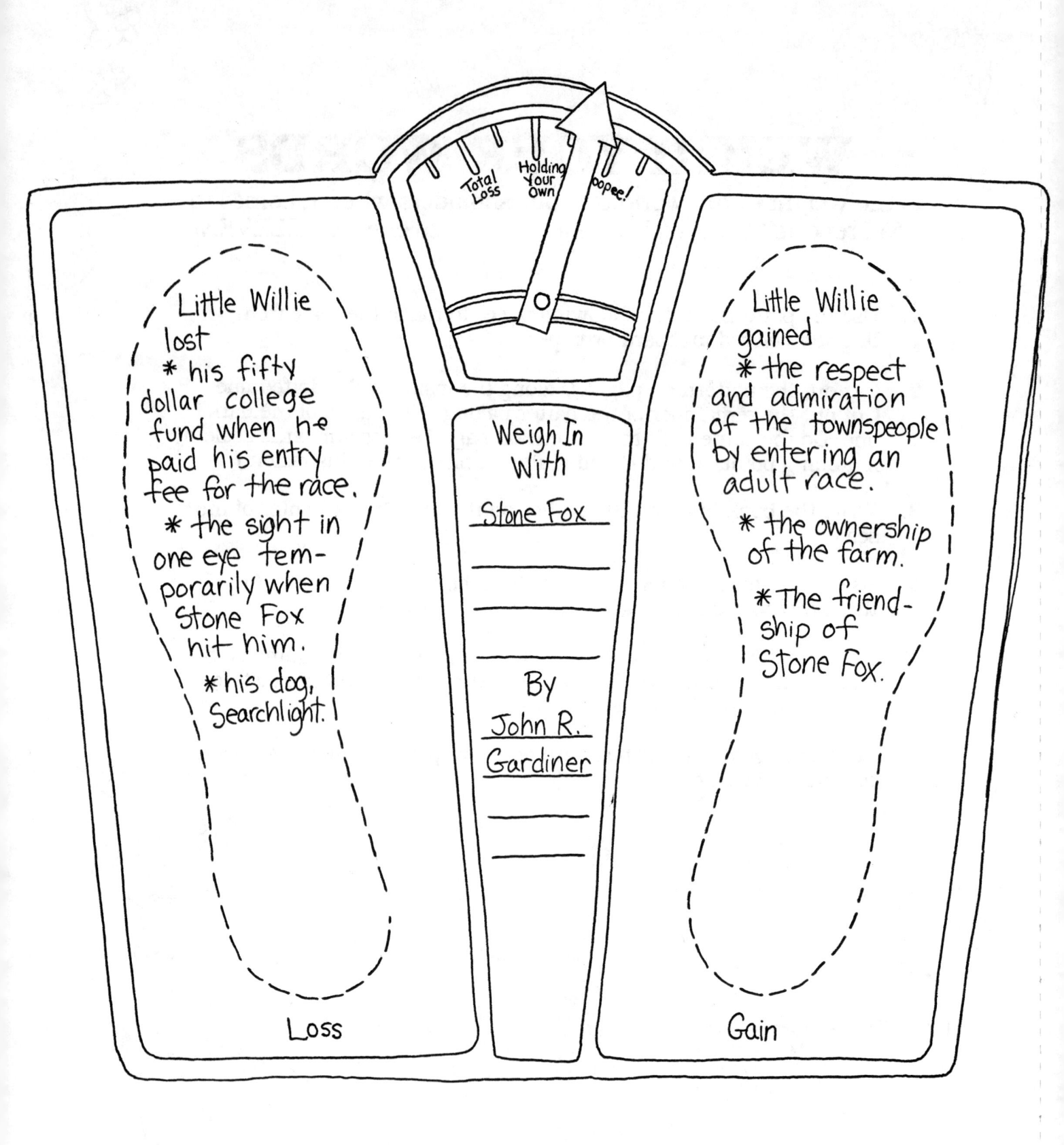

Scale dial labels: Total Loss | Holding Your Own | Whoopee!

Weigh In With
Stone Fox
By John R. Gardiner

Loss

Little Willie lost
* his fifty dollar college fund when he paid his entry fee for the race.
* the sight in one eye temporarily when Stone Fox hit him.
* his dog, Searchlight.

Gain

Little Willie gained
* the respect and admiration of the townspeople by entering an adult race.
* the ownership of the farm.
* The friendship of Stone Fox.

©1984 Incentive Publications, Inc., Nashville, TN. All rights reserved.

A ----

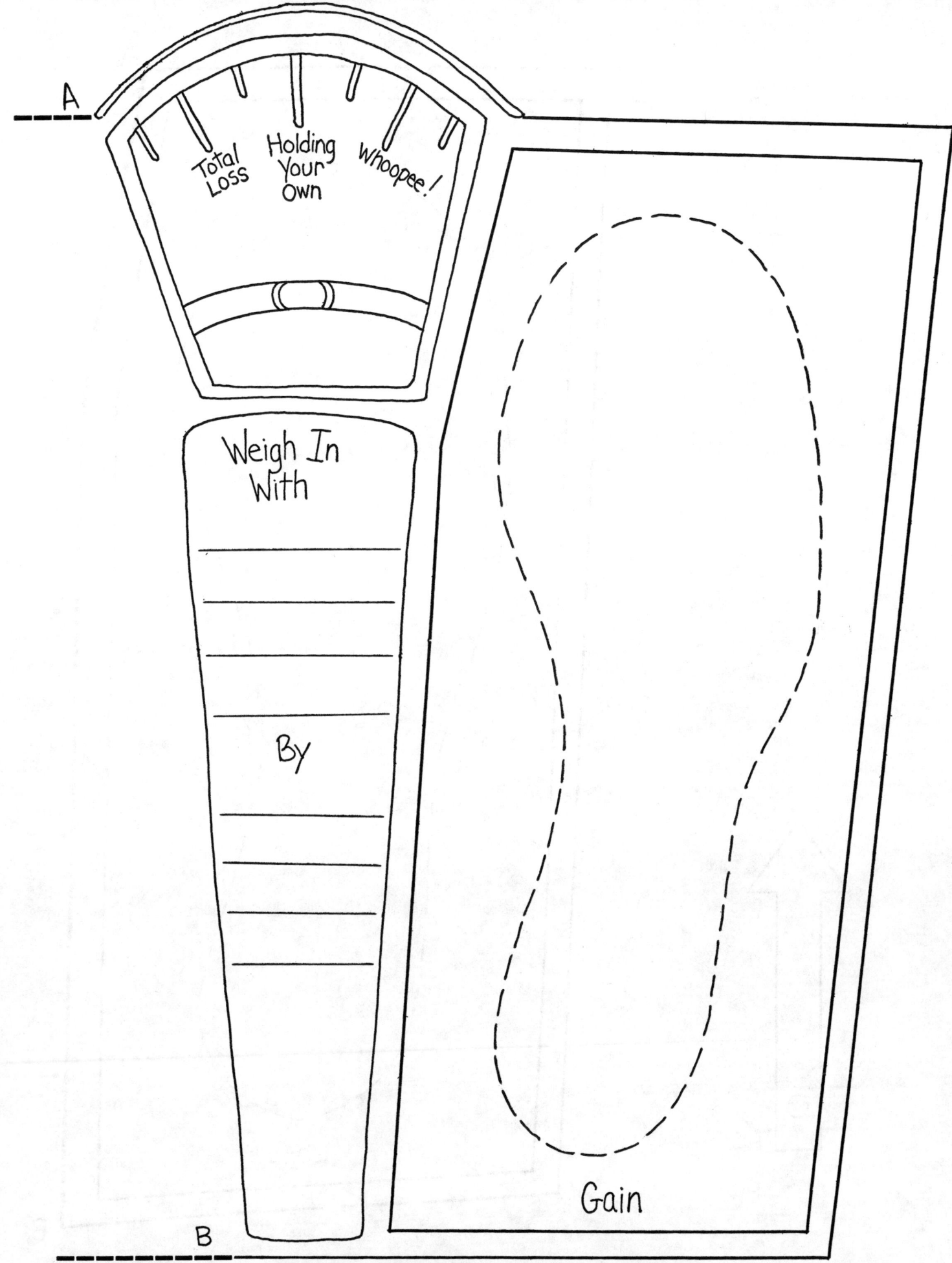

Total Loss   Holding Your Own   Whoopee!

Weigh In With

By

Gain

©1984 Incentive Publications, Inc., Nashville, TN. All rights reserved.

79

B ----

A

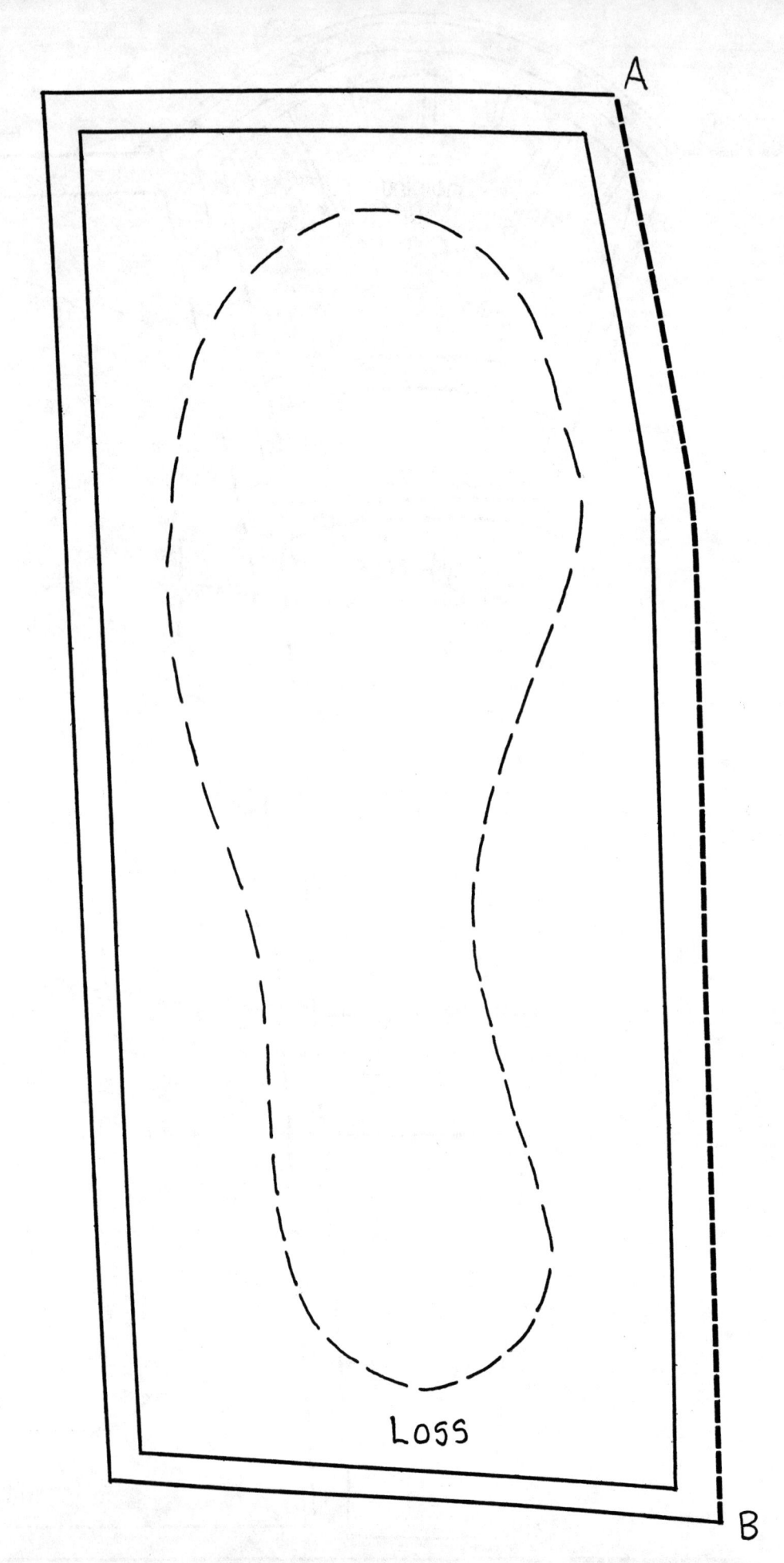

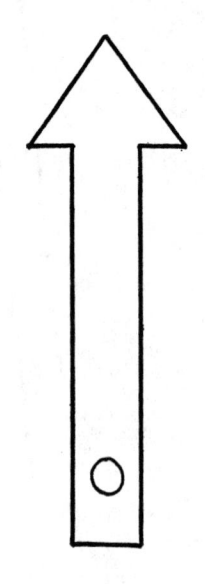

Loss

B

©1984 Incentive Publications, Inc., Nashville, TN. All rights reserved.

80

TO THE NTH DEGREE

If the thought of book reporting makes your temperature rise, this idea can help you keep your cool.

1. Use a piece of posterboard approximately 14 x 36 inches for the thermometer. Draw the thermometer shape in the center of the posterboard. Outline the shape in red. Write the book title and the author on the bulb of the thermometer.

2. Make slits two inches wide at the neck and the base of the thermometer. See the dotted lines of the illustration.

3. Use one-and-one-half inch wide elastic for the mercury. Cut a strip of elastic twice as long as the distance between the slits plus two inches. Color one half of the elastic red with a marker or dye.

4. Thread the elastic through the slits and staple together at the back. Do not staple elastic to the poster.

5. Use the phrase bank to show how the characters in the book behaved. Phrases denoting "hot" behavior belong at the top of the thermometer. "Cooler" phrases belong at the bottom. "Neutral" phrases are placed in the middle.

6. Move the red section of the elastic to the appropriate degree as you explain your book to the class.

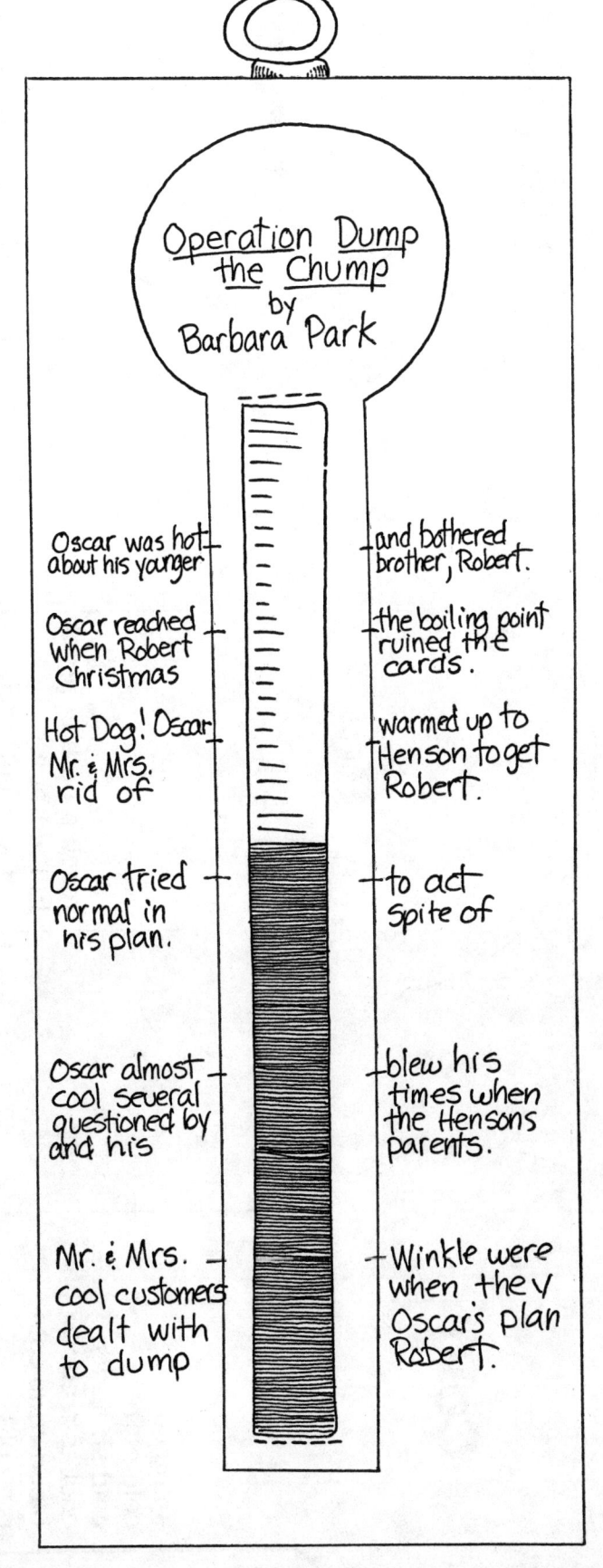

Operation Dump the Chump by Barbara Park

Oscar was hot / and bothered about his younger / brother, Robert.

Oscar reached / the boiling point when Robert / ruined the Christmas / cards.

Hot Dog! Oscar / warmed up to Mr. & Mrs. / Henson to get rid of / Robert.

Oscar tried / to act normal in / spite of his plan.

Oscar almost / blew his cool several / times when questioned by / the Hensons and his / parents.

Mr. & Mrs. / Winkle were cool customers / when they dealt with / Oscar's plan to dump / Robert.

81

Phrase Bank

Cold

- spine chilling
- cold stare
- cold shoulder
- cool as a cucumber
- blood runs cold
- out cold
- stop cold
- out in the cold
- cold feet
- cold fish
- throw cold water on
- cold turkey
- cool your heels
- cool off
- cold comfort

Hot

- reach a boiling point
- full of hot air
- hot and bothered
- hot around the collar
- hot potato
- on a hot seat
- in hot water
- warm up to
- hot headed
- Hot Dog!
- hot time
- warm as toast

Neutral

- hot and cold running water
- lukewarm
- normal
- tepid
- no change
- average
- indifferent
- middle ground

©1984 Incentive Publications, Inc., Nashville, TN. All rights reserved.

SEW BEE IT!

Don't go to pieces over book reporting! This project can sew up ideas that cover your book.

1. Use a twin-sized flat sheet for the quilt. Using a permanent marker, divide the center of the sheet into twelve 12-inch squares.

2. Using permanent markers, write the book title and the author in the bottom center square of the quilt. (Use permanent markers for all writing.)

3. Use fabric scraps to make appliques for important events, scenes, characters and/or symbols from the book. Patterns may be found in coloring books, pattern books, greeting cards, etc.

4. Glue a fabric applique to the center of each square.

5. On the border of the quilt, explain the meaning of each square or give a brief summary of the book.

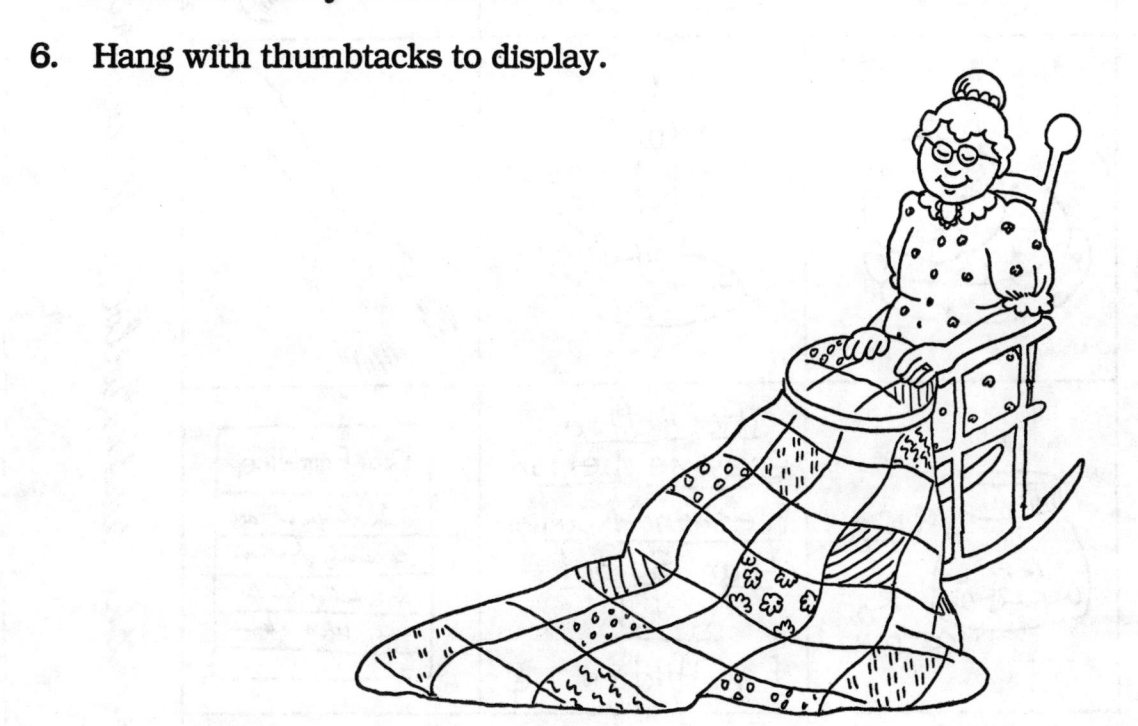

6. Hang with thumbtacks to display.

McNair discovered she was a witch when she was twelve. With her sister, Jeannie, as her Deputy, she dealt in magic. This produced strange results.

— Alison

SINGLE FILE

This project is top drawer! Call your characters to order with this personnel file.

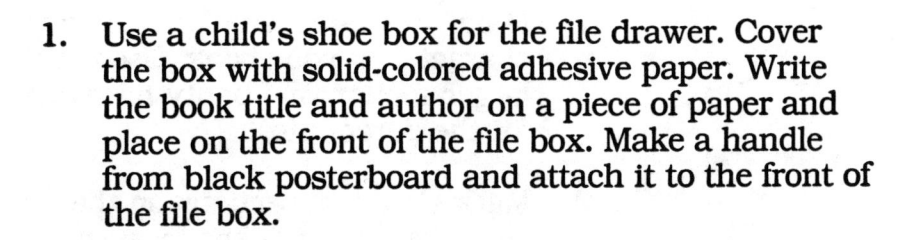

1. Use a child's shoe box for the file drawer. Cover the box with solid-colored adhesive paper. Write the book title and author on a piece of paper and place on the front of the file box. Make a handle from black posterboard and attach it to the front of the file box.

2. Make a 3 x 5 inch file folder from tagboard for each main character. Write the character's name on the file tab.

3. On a 3 x 5 inch index card, briefly tell about the character's role in the book.

4. Inside the folder, include the index card, pictures, articles and advertisements of items, places or people that are important or of interest in the character's life.

HAPPY LANDINGS

Jump into good book reporting with this sky-high idea! Characters who take a chance or need security will land feet first with this project.

1. Make one parachute for each main character in your book. Use the larger section of a panty hose egg for the parachute.

2. Mark six equal sections on the egg. Use a permanent marker.

3. Punch holes in the lower edge of the egg at each dividing line. Punch a hole in the center top of the egg.

4. Use the pattern to make a figure from tagboard or posterboard for each parachute. Decorate appropriately. Write the character's name on the front of the figure.

5. Make two 8 x 18 inch clouds from white posterboard. On one cloud, write the book title and author's name.

6. On the second cloud, write a brief account for each character, explaining how that character took a chance or felt insecure. Be sure to include a statement telling how the character resolved the situation.

7. Punch two holes in the tops of the clouds and secure to a coat hanger so that the hanger hook extends above the clouds.

8. Punch evenly spaced holes in the bottom of the clouds to hang the figures.

9. Use six 4-inch lengths of thread for each character's parachute lines. Thread each thread through a different hole in the egg. Knot the thread on the outside of the egg.

10. Gather three strands of thread together at the bottom and knot. Tape or staple one hand of a figure to the three knotted strands. Tape or staple the remaining three knotted strands to the other hand.

11. Thread a string through the hole in the top center of each egg. Knot one end inside the top of the egg. Secure the remaining ends to a hole in the bottom of the cloud.

12. Hang as a mobile.

©1984 Incentive Publications, Inc., Nashville, TN. All rights reserved.

SHOOT OUT

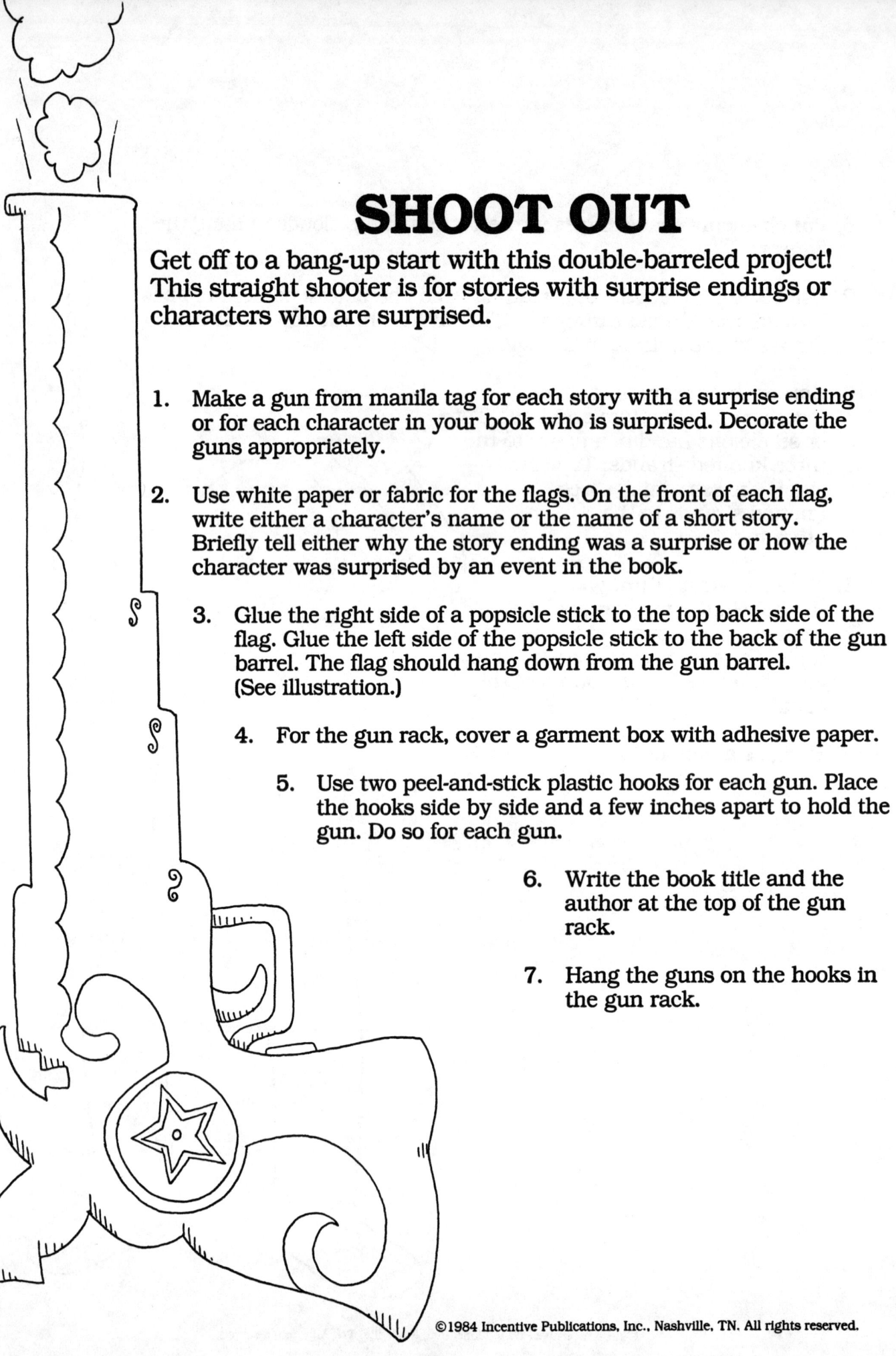

Get off to a bang-up start with this double-barreled project! This straight shooter is for stories with surprise endings or characters who are surprised.

1. Make a gun from manila tag for each story with a surprise ending or for each character in your book who is surprised. Decorate the guns appropriately.

2. Use white paper or fabric for the flags. On the front of each flag, write either a character's name or the name of a short story. Briefly tell either why the story ending was a surprise or how the character was surprised by an event in the book.

3. Glue the right side of a popsicle stick to the top back side of the flag. Glue the left side of the popsicle stick to the back of the gun barrel. The flag should hang down from the gun barrel. (See illustration.)

4. For the gun rack, cover a garment box with adhesive paper.

5. Use two peel-and-stick plastic hooks for each gun. Place the hooks side by side and a few inches apart to hold the gun. Do so for each gun.

6. Write the book title and the author at the top of the gun rack.

7. Hang the guns on the hooks in the gun rack.

©1984 Incentive Publications, Inc., Nashville, TN. All rights reserved.

PECOS BILL
by Nancy A. Lyman

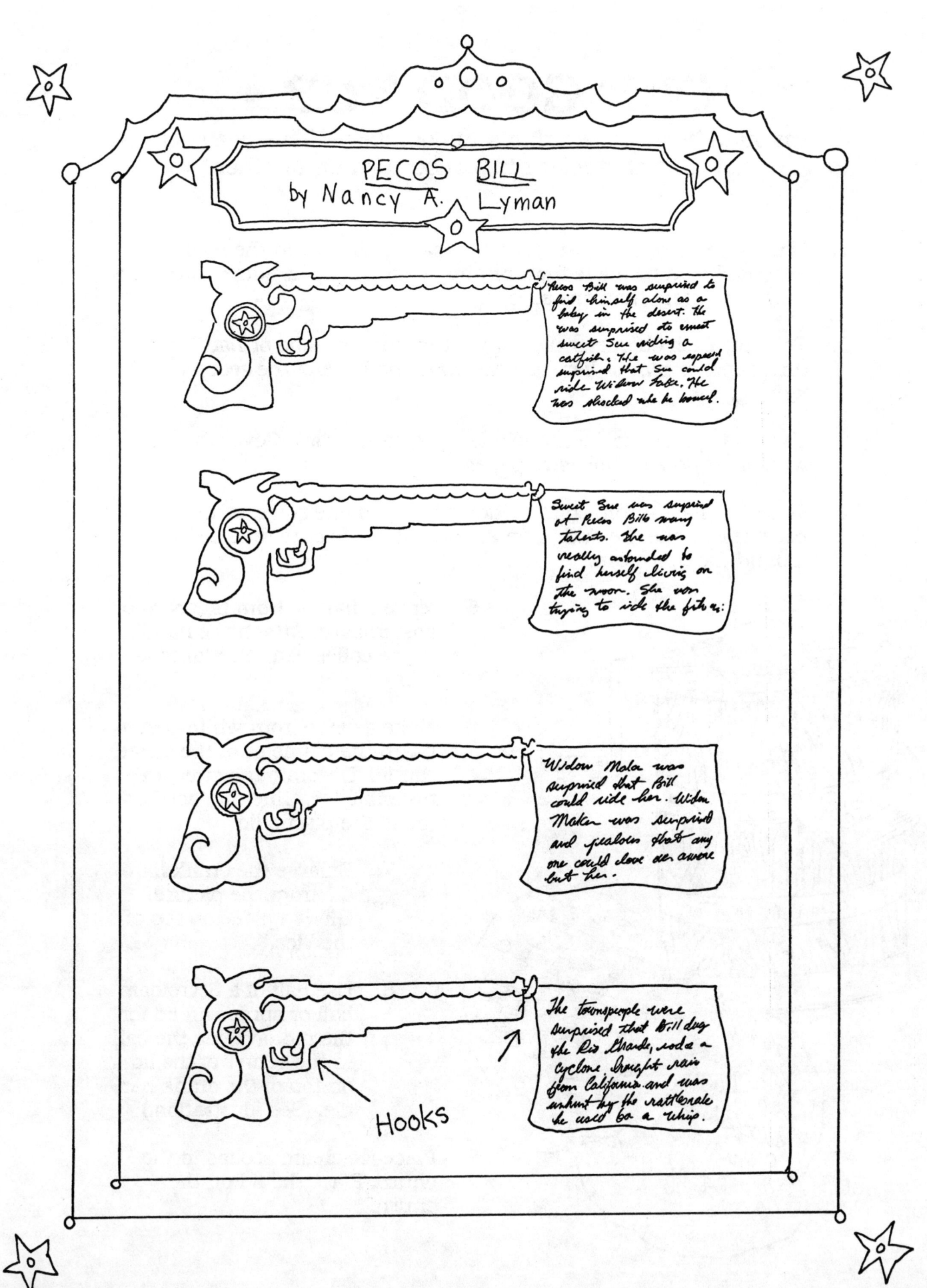

Pecos Bill was surprised to find himself alone as a baby in the desert. He was surprised to meet Sweet Sue riding a catfish. He was especially surprised that Sue could ride Widow Maker. He was shocked when he bounced.

Sweet Sue was surprised at Pecos Bill's many talents. She was really astounded to find herself living on the moon. She was trying to ride the fish.

Widow Maker was surprised that Bill could ride her. Widow Maker was surprised and jealous that any one could love or admire but her.

The townspeople were surprised that Bill dug the Rio Grande, rode a cyclone, brought rain from California, and was unhurt by the rattlesnake he used for a whip.

Hooks

ONE GOOD TURN

Churn out a book project that's in good taste. This is a cool way to show how one character did a good turn for another.

1. Make a scoop of ice cream for each main character in the book. Scoops should be made from brightly colored paper. Some characters may need more than one scoop.

2. Tell how each character did a good turn for someone or had a good turn done for him or her. Use the front and back of the scoop for writing.

3. Use a one-pound coffee can for the ice-cream churn. Cover the can with wood-grained adhesive paper.

4. Make the staves from construction paper. On one stave, write the book title. Write the author on another stave. Secure the staves around the coffee can.

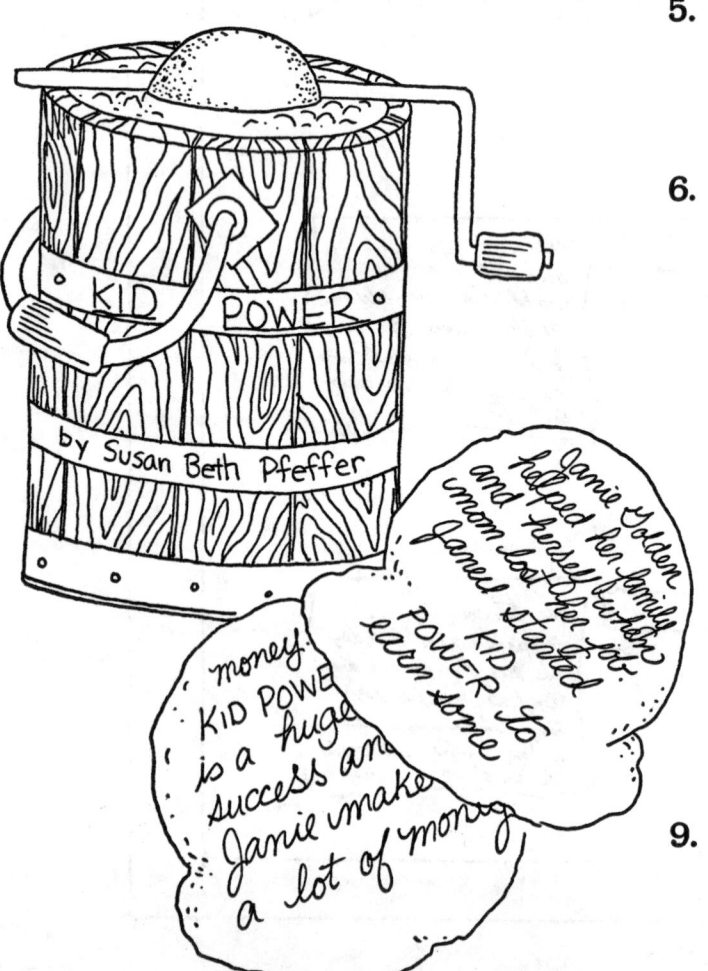

5. Make a handle from tagboard or posterboard. Attach the handle to the coffee can. (See illustration.)

6. Make a circle from white posterboard the diameter of the coffee can lid. Decorate the circle to resemble ice. Glue the "ice" on top of the plastic lid.

7. Enlarge the crank handle from the picture. Glue in place on top of the "ice."

8. Use half of a Styrofoam ball or spray-can lid for the motor. Glue the ball in the center of the lid on top of the crank handle. (See illustration.)

9. Place ice-cream scoops in the churn. Place the lid on the churn.

SOMETHING'S FISHY

Hooked on a suspense-filled book? This book project will tip the scales in your favor!

1. Make a fish for each of the main characters in your book. Use any of the following fish patterns. Punch a hole in each fish near its mouth.

2. On each fish, write the name of a character. Explain how that character was caught in a strange situation or how the character caught someone else in interesting circumstances.

3. Decorate the fish appropriately. Make sure the decorations do not interfere with the writing.

4. Use a dowel rod for the fishing pole. Tie a piece of yarn, string or ribbon to one end of the dowel rod as a fishing line.

5. Write the book title and author on the pole.

6. Tie the opposite end of the fishing line to a metal shower curtain ring. Slip the fish onto the ring.

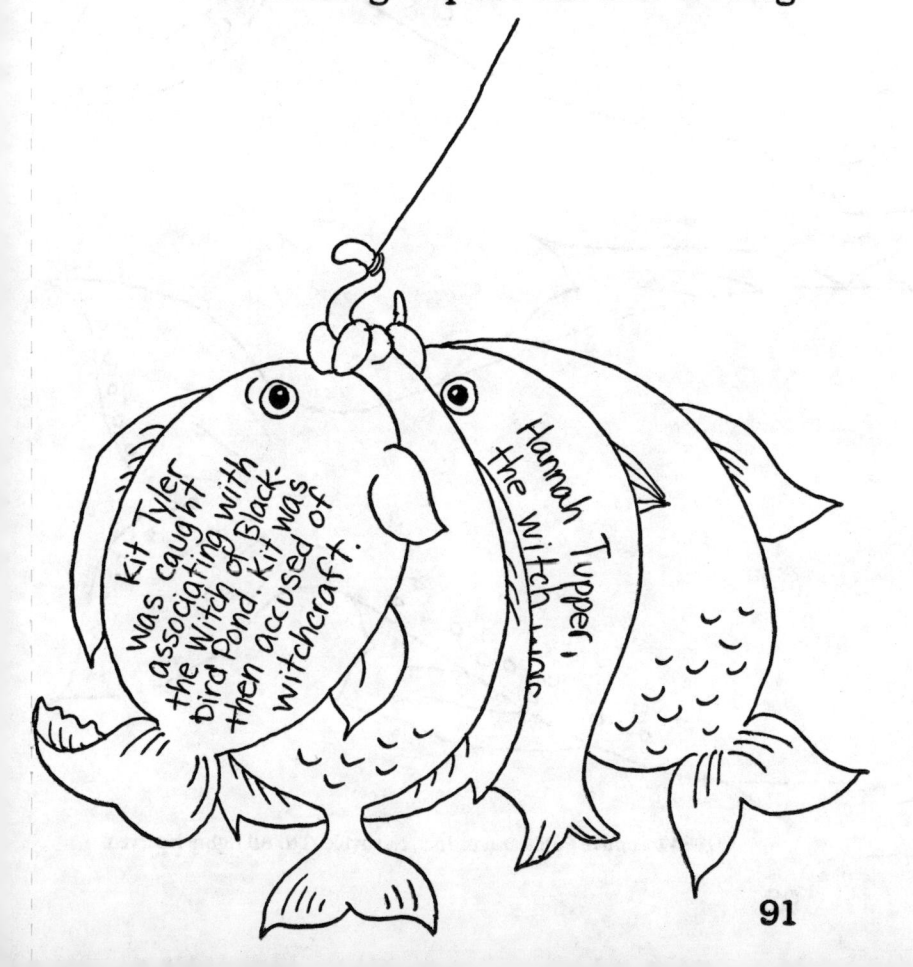

©1984 Incentive Publications, Inc., Nashville, TN. All rights reserved.

92

IF THE SHOE FITS

This idea will be a real shoo-in for book characters who have been either lucky or unlucky. Use these horseshoes to make a "ringer" of a book project.

1. Decide how the main characters in your book have been lucky or unlucky. Make a horseshoe from posterboard for each character using the pattern.
2. Write a character's name on each horseshoe and explain how that character was lucky or unlucky. You may need more than one shoe for each character.
3. Use a 18 x 6 inch piece of green Styrofoam for the horseshoe court. Use a dowel rod for the horseshoe stake. Write the book title and author on the stake. Press the stake into the Styrofoam four inches from the back edge.
4. If a horseshoe depicts a lucky incident, place it around the stake as a "ringer." If it depicts an unlucky event, place the horseshoe away from the stake.

©1984 Incentive Publications, Inc., Nashville, TN. All rights reserved.

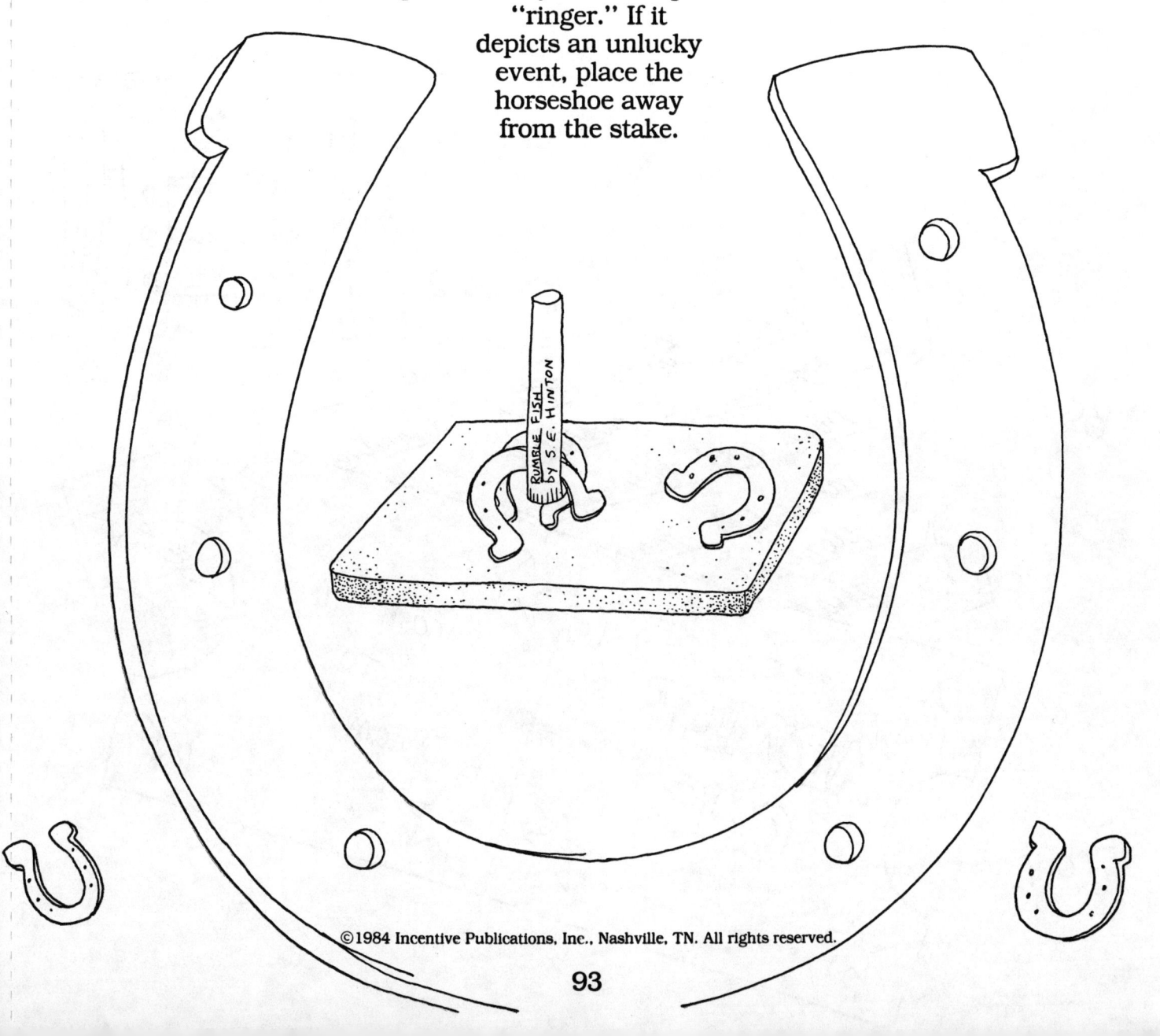

93

TICKET-TAKER

This idea will provide a one-way ticket to book reporting success!

1. Use the pattern to make tickets from brightly colored paper or tagboard. Make a ticket for each place a character wants or needs to go.

2. On the front of each ticket, write the destination of the character and the mode of travel. (See illustration.)

3. Draw lines on the back of each ticket. On these lines, explain why the character wants or needs to travel to that destination.

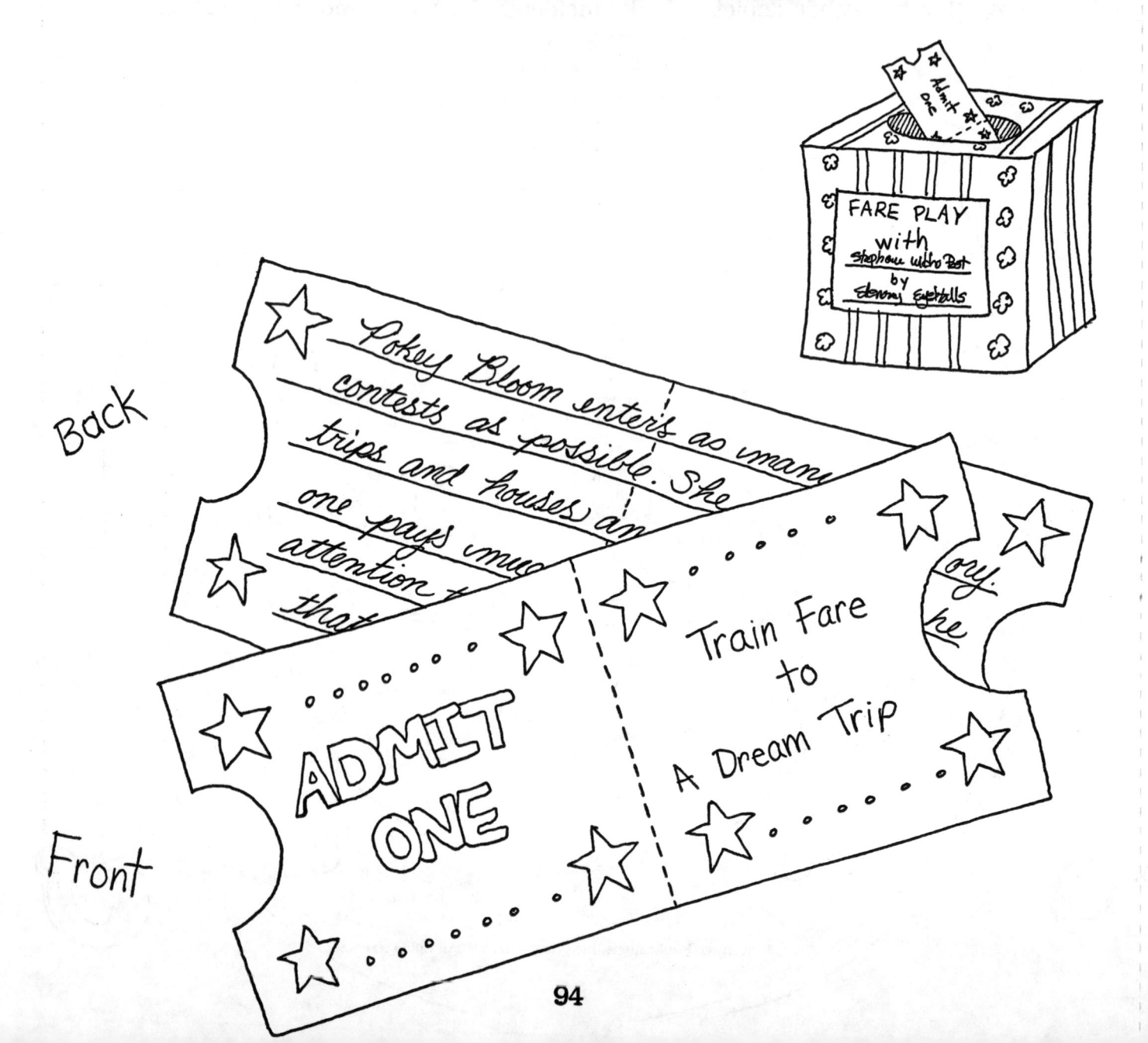

4. Cover a square tissue box with adhesive-backed paper. Make a "FARE PLAY" label for the front of the box. Write the book title and the author on the label.

5. Fold each ticket in half. Insert the tickets in the ticket-taker's box.

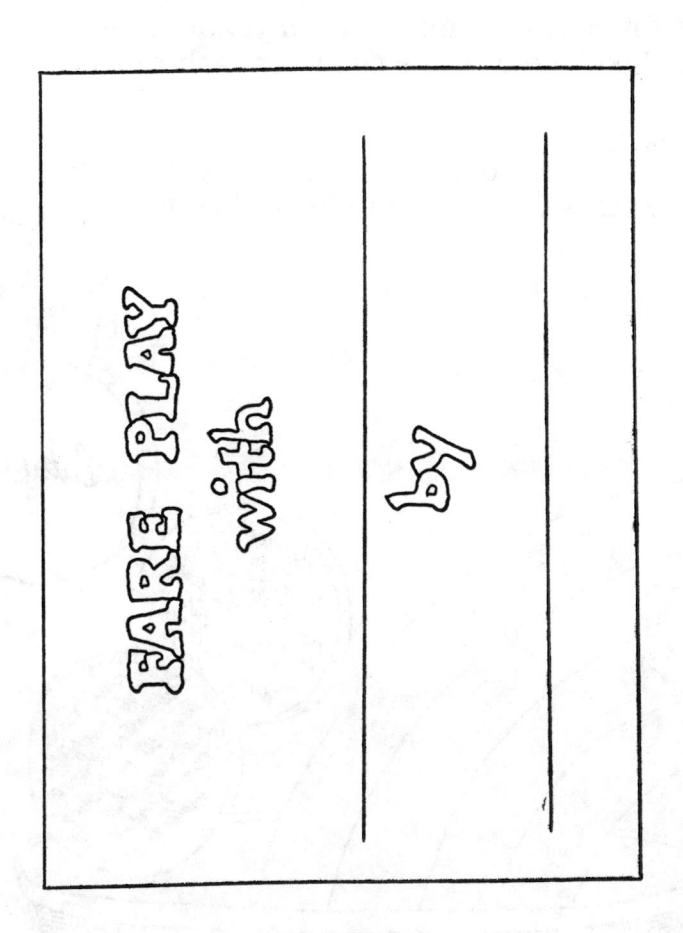

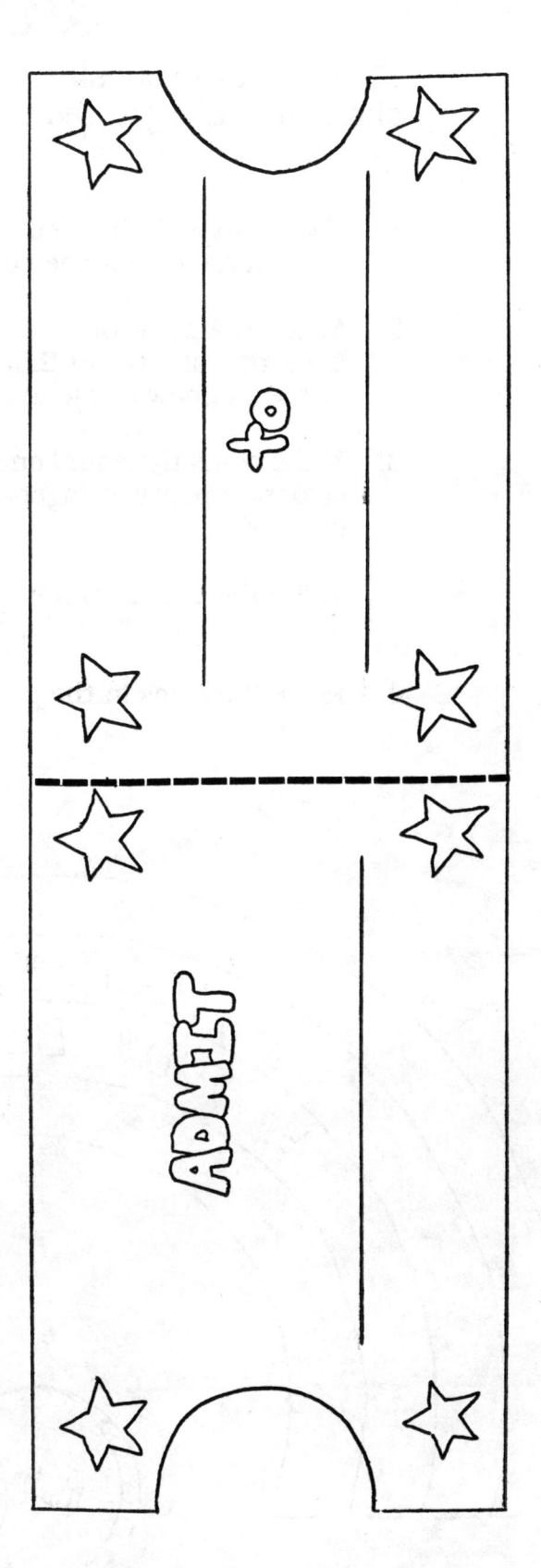

FARE PLAY with

by

ADMIT

©1984 Incentive Publications, Inc., Nashville, TN. All rights reserved.

95

POT LUCK

Thank your lucky stars for this project that shows how characters are granted their wishes.

1. Use a large plastic container for the pot. Spray the container black. Make a handle for the pot.

2. Make a rainbow of multi-colored tagboard or posterboard. Write the book title and the author on the rainbow. Staple the right bottom end of the rainbow to the inside back of the "pot." (See illustration.)

3. Make coins three-and-one-half inches in diameter from yellow construction paper or tagboard. Make one or more coins for each main character.

    Write the character's name on one side of the coin. On the other side of the coin, tell how the character got what he or she wished for.

4. Place the coins in the pot.

ABRACADABRA

Get a jack-rabbit start on book reporting with this tricky idea. Your students will be bewitched with this project meant for books about magic or books with magical events.

1. Use a two-pound coffee can for the magician's hat. Cover the can with black kraft paper.

2. Make the hat brim from a black posterboard circle nine inches in diameter. Cut a circle five inches in diameter out of the center. Wedge this brim down over the open top of the can. (See illustration.)

3. Make a rabbit for each magical event in the book or each trick explained in a book of magic.

4. On the rabbit's book, write the name of the character(s) who participated in the magical event or the title of the magic trick.

5. On the lines, explain the event or the trick.

6. Write the book title and the author's name on another rabbit's book. Place all the rabbits in the hat.

97

TOAST OF THE TOWN

Use this upper-crust idea for book characters who deserve some praise! You'll discover which side your book reporting bread is buttered on!

1. Use a one-pound cracker box for the toaster. Cover the "toaster" with aluminum foil. Cut four slits exactly the width of the toast in the top of the toaster.

2. Use posterboard to make four pieces of toast. On each piece of toast, write the name of a book character and tell how that character earned praise. You may also praise a character on one side of the toast and "roast" the character for his or her misdeeds on the opposite side. Place the toast in the toaster so that at least half of it shows above the top. (See illustration.)

3. Make handles from black posterboard and attach them to the sides of the toaster.

4. Write the book title and the author on the base of the toaster.

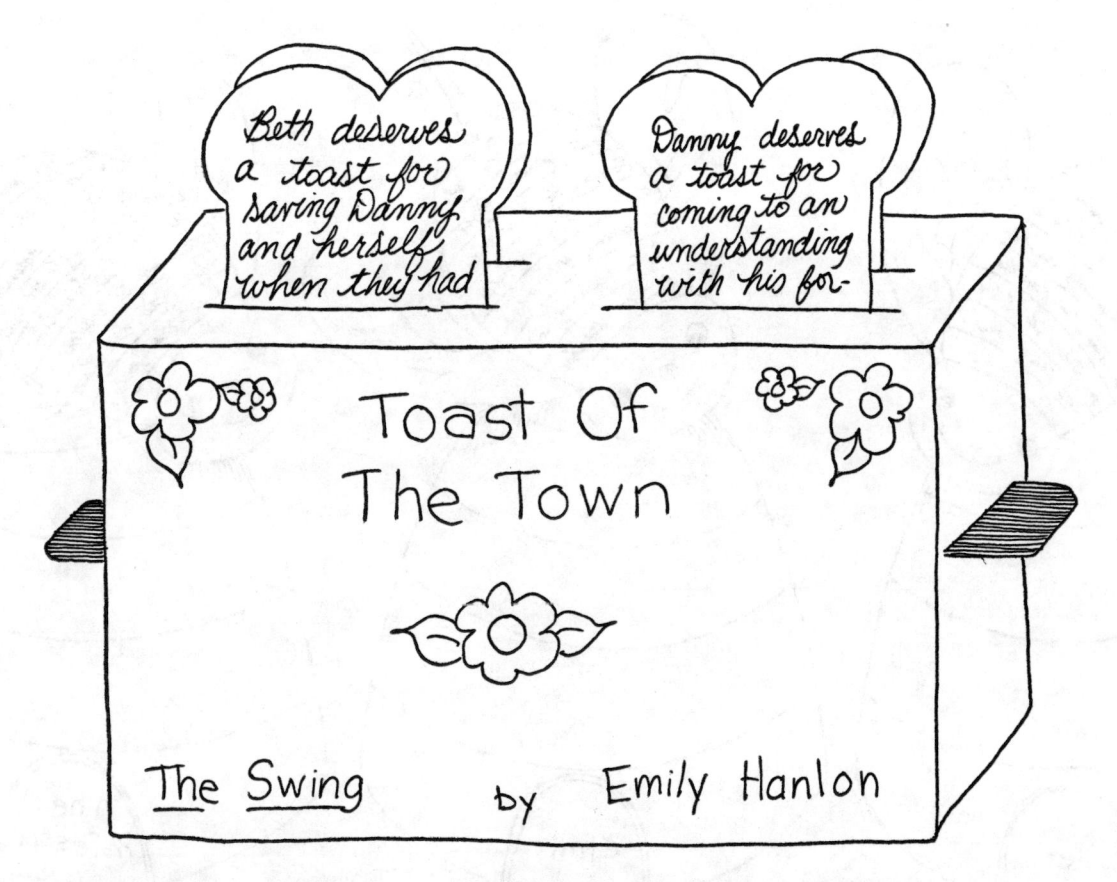

MAKE A BEELINE

Got a bee in your bonnet about book reporting? Dive into this project — it will make a bee-liever out of you when you show how the characters in your book were busy as bees!

1. Use the larger portion of a panty hose egg to make a hive for each main book character. Make parallel lines around each hive with a permanent black marker. (See illustration.) Make a door at the base of each hive. Write the name of a character on the door of each hive.

2. Use the bee pattern to make a bee from tagboard for each main character in the book. On the stripes of the bee, tell how the character kept busy in the story.

from *Sea Pup* by Archie Binns

3. Place double-faced tape on the back of each bee. Attach the bee to the top of the appropriate hive.

4. Use the pattern to make a beekeeper from tagboard. Decorate appropriately. Write the book title and author on the beekeeper. Attach a tongue depressor or popsicle stick to the back of the beekeeper.

5. Use a piece of green Styrofoam for the base of the hives. Press the hives into the Styrofoam in a row. Insert the beekeeper into the Styrofoam behind the hives.

©1984 Incentive Publications, Inc., Nashville, TN. All rights reserved.

©1984 Incentive Publications, Inc., Nashville, TN. All rights reserved.

HEAD START

If your book reporting has become "old hat," try this heads up idea.

1. Cut four pieces of posterboard measuring 12 x 2 inches. Cut four more pieces of posterboard measuring 6 x 2 inches. Cover all the poster strips with wood-grain adhesive paper.

2. Staple the strips of posterboard together to make a hatrack. (See illustration.)

3. Use peel-and-stick utility hooks for the hat hangers.

4. Characters wear different hats in their roles in stories. The hats may be connected with their jobs, hobbies, travels or feelings. Make hats from tagboard, posterboard or construction paper appropriate for the main character in your book. On the back of each hat, explain the importance of the hat to the character.

5. Hang the hats on the hooks. Hang the rack to display.

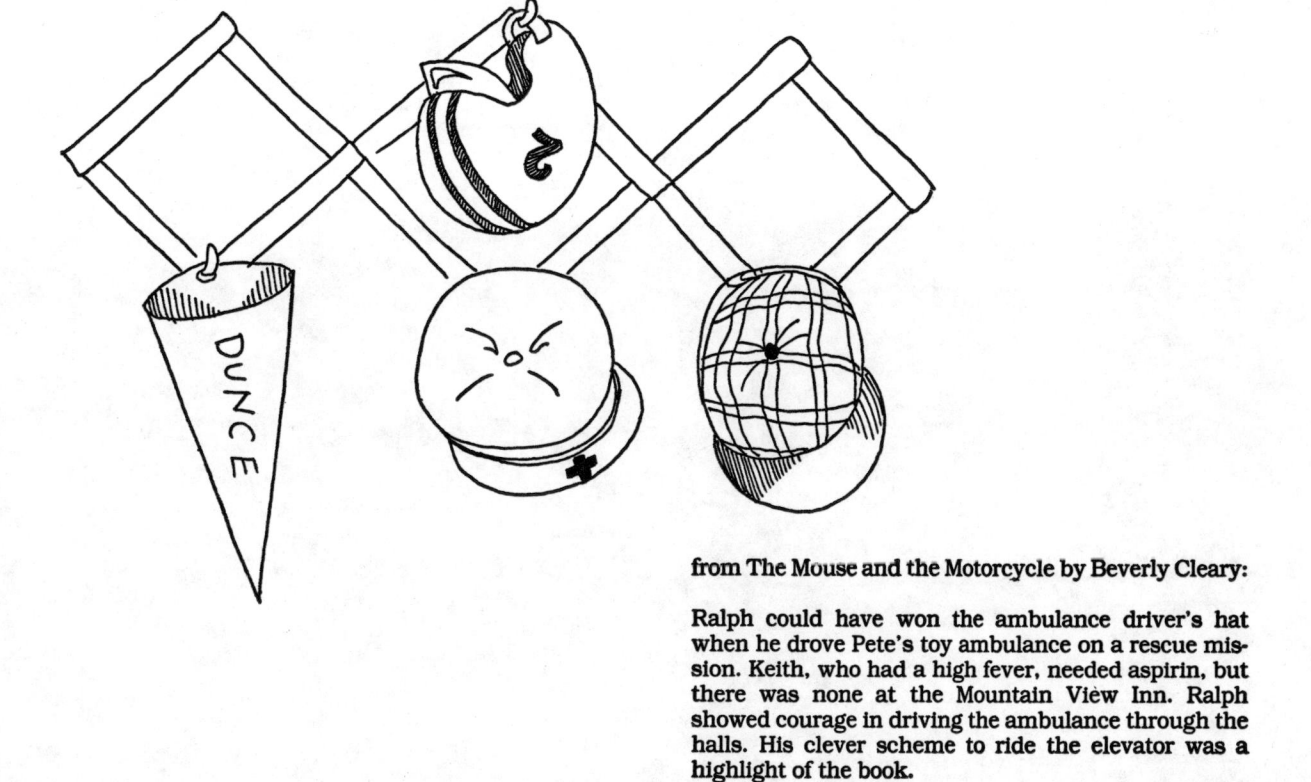

from The Mouse and the Motorcycle by Beverly Cleary:

Ralph could have won the ambulance driver's hat when he drove Pete's toy ambulance on a rescue mission. Keith, who had a high fever, needed aspirin, but there was none at the Mountain View Inn. Ralph showed courage in driving the ambulance through the halls. His clever scheme to ride the elevator was a highlight of the book.

Appendix

CRITIC'S CHOICE

BOOK: _____

_____

AUTHOR: _____

ILLUSTRATOR: _____

_____

GENRE: _____

INTEREST LEVEL: _____

ILLUSTRATIONS

The cover of this book is

_____ eyecatching, _____ mediocre, _____ boring.

Explain your choice. _____

_____

_____

_____   _____

- yes   no   The book is illustrated. If yes, circle one: oils, pastels, watercolor, pen and ink sketches, photos, other: _____
- yes   no   Illustrations are near the paragraphs they illustrate.
- yes   no   Illustrations are accurate. They depict the descriptions in the book.
- yes   no   Illustrations appeal to the interest level for which the book is intended.

©1984 Incentive Publications, Inc., Nashville, TN. All rights reserved.

STYLE

yes   no   The reader can easily detect the setting. If so, state:

TIME:_____

PLACE:_____

_____

yes   no   Characters have well-developed personalities.

yes   no   The story has a well-developed plot. If so, state:

BEGINNING: _____

_____,

MIDDLE: _____

_____,

END: _____

_____.

yes   no   The story moves along at a good pace.

USE

yes   no   This story could be used in other subject areas. If so, circle the appropriate subjects: Math, Science, Social Studies, Art, Music, P.E., Other: _____.

yes   no   This book would be a good addition to a school library. If so, why? _____

_____

_____

Have you read other books

_____ on the same subject, _____ by the same author,

_____ in the same series, _____ of the same genre?

If so, list them. _____

_____

_____

_____

_____

How do they compare? _____

_____

_____

_____

PERSONAL COMMENTS _____

_____

_____

_____

_____

TEACHER'S RESPONSE _____

_____

_____

_____

_____

_____

©1984 Incentive Publications, Inc., Nashville, TN. All rights reserved.

EVALUATION

Student   **Teacher**

___ ___ Provided essentials without telling the entire story.
___ ___ Used meaningful vocabulary.
___ ___ Followed directions or adapted the project to suit the book.
___ ___ Obvious that the book was read.

APPEARANCE

___ ___ Neat and attractive.
___ ___ Working parts do work.
___ ___ Shows effort and time well spent.

MECHANICS

___ ___ Correct grammar usage.
___ ___ Correct punctuation usage.
___ ___ Correct spelling.

PRESENTATION

___ ___ Spoke clearly to the audience.
___ ___ Project displayed visibly to the audience.
___ ___ Presented within the time allotted.
___ ___ Kept audience attention.

PLANNING

NAME _____

BOOK TITLE _____

AUTHOR _____

PROJECT _____

I need these supplies: _____

I will need help from _____ who will _____.

I will pace myself:

MON.	TUES.	WED.	THURS.	FRI.

MON.	TUES.	WED.	THURS.	FRI.

©1984 Incentive Publications, Inc., Nashville, TN. All rights reserved.

MAKE IT SNAPPY

1. Make a book jacket depicting the characters, setting and theme of your book.

2. Use photographs and captions to make a family album or scrapbook based on your book.

3. Make a home movie or filmstrip.

4. Make a comic strip.

5. Make an illustrated time line for historical books.

6. Construct a diorama.

7. Construct a mobile.

8. Construct a sand table.

9. Make clay, soap, wood or plaster models.

10. Make a collection or keepsake box of souvenirs from the story.

11. Make a mural.

12. Give a flannel board talk.

13. Make a collage.

14. Draw several clocks showing the times of important events.

15. Make a bulletin board or learning center.

16. Construct a jigsaw puzzle based on the book.

17. Design a coloring book around the characters and events.

18. Make a board game.

19. Create a set of bumper stickers based on the characters and events

20. Make a series of bookmarks with appropriate shapes. Choose wise sayings from the book to write on the bookmarks.

21. Make a word search or crossword puzzle.

22. Make a wanted poster for an appropriate character.

23. Make a family tree.

24. Design a set of T-shirts to suit the characters.

SOUND EFFECTS

1. Broadcast a book review.

2. Tell the story to musical accompaniment that suits the mood of the book.

3. Tape record an important conversation or excerpts from the book.

4. Conduct an interview between the author and characters or between you and a character or between two characters.

5. Make a nomination speech for your book for either the Caldecott or Newbery Award.

6. Make a brief oral report on why this book should never be spoiled by a book report.

SHOW OFF

1. Dress as one of the characters and tell about yourself or tell about the other characters from your point of view.

2. Produce a quiz show.

3. Give a TV presentation or film preview of the book.

4. Create a puppet show using stick, finger, glove or hand puppets.

5. Create a 10 to 15 minute soap opera episode based on your story.

6. Hold a panel discussion or debate when several students have read the same book.

7. Retell the story to a group of younger children.

8. Invite three celebrities (three others who have read the book). Make an invitation so that the time, place and kind of party are suitable to the book.

9. Hold an auction. Auction off important objects from the book.

10. Create a game show based on your book.

WRITER'S CRAMP

1. Write a book review giving unfavorable opinions.

2. Write a movie script for part of the book.

3. Write a different ending.

4. Write a letter to a friend or a librarian to recommend the book.

5. Write and draw a rebus story based on the book.

6. Think up a new adventure, incident or experience to add to the book.

7. Make word puzzles based on the book.

8. Make a newspaper. Include events that could have occurred and when and where the story took place.

9. Develop a dictionary for a character in the book. It should include words that he or she particularly liked to use as well as definitions that character would have given the words.

10. Make an original reference book from factual information found in the book.

11. Add additional stanzas to favorite poems in a poetry book.

12. Write a job wanted ad for the main characters in your book.

13. Write lost and found columns for objects and people in the book.

14. Make an autograph book for the main character.

15. Write a series of letters or postcards from one character to another.

16. Write a series of "Dear Abby" letters from characters. Answer with your advice.

17. Devise a horoscope for the main characters.

18. Write several diary entries for the main characters.

19. Make a test (with answer key for the teacher and other students to take).

20. Make a reading tablecloth or quilt.

As a follow-up to project presentations, use these attention-getters. These ideas may be used with large or small groups. They are primarily designed as closure activities when the class book reports are all completed.

LOOKING BACK

The teacher writes the name of many characters from the class reports on 3 x 5 inch cards. She or he tapes one card to each student's back. The student does not know which character's name is on his or her back. The students may ask each other questions that may be answered yes or no to uncover his or her identity.

SMART COOKIE

Each student is given an empty fortune cookie and a blank strip of paper. The student writes a fortune suitable for the main character of the book. (Example: You will take a long train trip to Connecticut. [from *The Cricket in Times Square*.]) The student places the strip inside a cookie and the cookies are placed in a bowl. Each student takes a cookie and tries to guess the character's name.

SCAVENGER HUNT

Have each student bring to class a item representative of the main character in his or her book. The teacher hides the items in the classroom. Each student gets a list of all the hidden items. The class is allowed time to discover the objects without touching them or revealing their hiding places. On the list, the student writes the name of the character or book that the item represents and the place where it was found.

READING RELAY

Divide the class into two or more equal groups. The teacher lists on the chalkboard the characters or the events from the books read by the class (one list for each group of students). In relay fashion, the students go to the chalkboard and write the names of the books beside the events or the characters. Prizes may be awarded for the winning group.

CHECK IT OUT!

Have your students choose a reading partner as an opponent. Give each "team" a duplicated checkerboard. As each student reads a book, he or she records the title and author on a "blank" space on his or her side of the checkerboard. The first student to fill up his or her side of the board wins.

©1984 Incentive Publications, Inc., Nashville, TN. All rights reserved.

MARK MY WORD

Mark my word, reading is fun! Duplicate the bookmarks on tagboard. Each student can decorate the bookmark to resemble himself or herself. Attach a strip of notebook or tablet paper to the front of the bookmark. Staple at the "X." As the student reads the book, he or she lists it on the paper to keep track of the total books read.

©1984 Incentive Publications, Inc., Nashville, TN. All rights reserved.

HOLIDAY IDEAS

Have a Heart, Read a Book!

For Valentine's Day, have each group (or student if you have the room) make a giant heart mobile. Lace together two construction paper hearts. Decorate the outside of the heart. Insert a coat hanger and hang.

For each book that is read, the student earns a Valentine. His or her name, the author's name and the book title are written on the blank side of a Valentine. Valentines are dropped into the giant heart until Valentine's Day. Winners might receive a prize.

Punch holes in the heart and lace with bright yarn.

Eggstra Reading!

At Eastertime, make the most of all those panty hose eggs you've been collecting! Each reading group should have an Easter basket. Have each student decorate an egg with Easter or flower stickers. A peel-and-stick label may be used to identify each student's egg.

As books are read, the student places a construction paper chick, rabbit or egg in his or her egg. The day before Easter vacation, each student counts the contents of his or her egg. The winner in each group might receive a prize.

Gift-wrapped Reading

At Christmastime, have each student wrap a small box in Christmas paper and place a gift tag on it with his or her name from Santa Claus. A slit is then made in each box. Boxes are placed beneath the classroom tree. As books are read, the student takes a gift tag, writes the title and author of his or her book on it and slides the tag through the slit into the box. On the last day of school before the Christmas holidays, students open their boxes and count the gift tags. The student reading the most books receives a gift from Santa.

Fly High with Reading!

In the springtime, when kite flying season is upon us, have students make kites. Hang them as mobiles in the classroom. Students can add a tailpiece recording the book title and the author as each book is read.

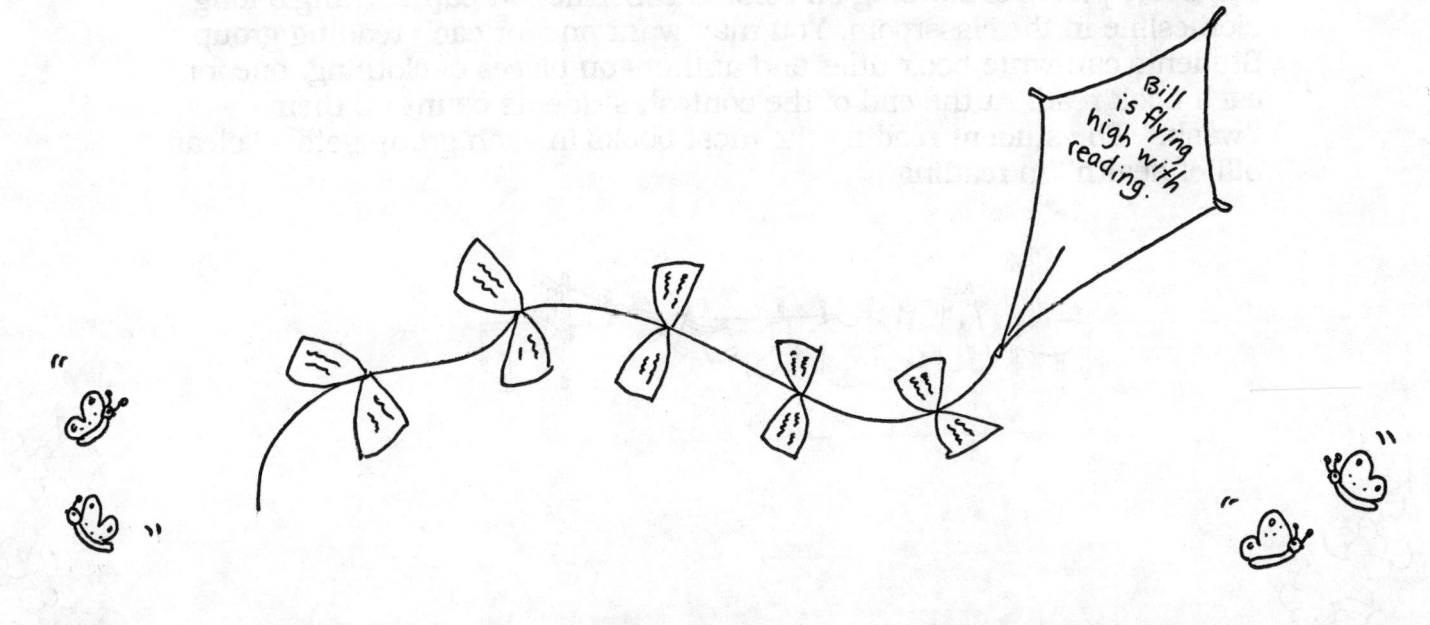

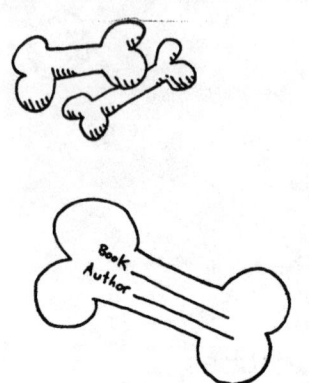

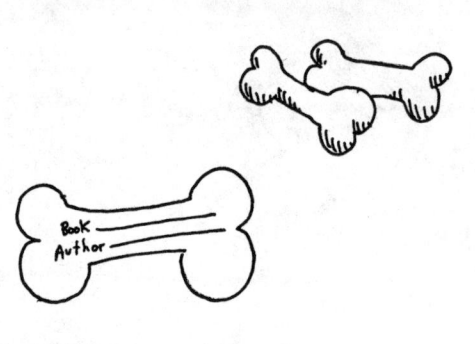

I'll Be Doggone. Reading Is Fun!

Display a large stuffed dog. At his feet, place a large feeding bowl. You might want to use three small bowls — one for each group. As students read, the titles and authors are written on bone shapes. Bones are then placed in the bowl until the contest is over.

Build-a-Bear

As each book is read, students write the title and author on a bear part that has been duplicated on tan, brown or white (for polar and panda bears) construction paper. When students have read six books, they have a bear. Staple or brad the parts together. Punch a hole in the head and loop yarn, thread or string through the hole to make a mobile. This is easily done with most animals.

Reading Is Our Hang-up!

Duplicate pieces of clothing on colored construction paper. Hang a long clothesline in the classroom. You may want one for each reading group. Students can write book titles and authors on pieces of clothing, one for each book read. At the end of the contest, students count up their "wash." The student reading the most books in each group gets a "clean bill of health" in reading.

REMINDERS

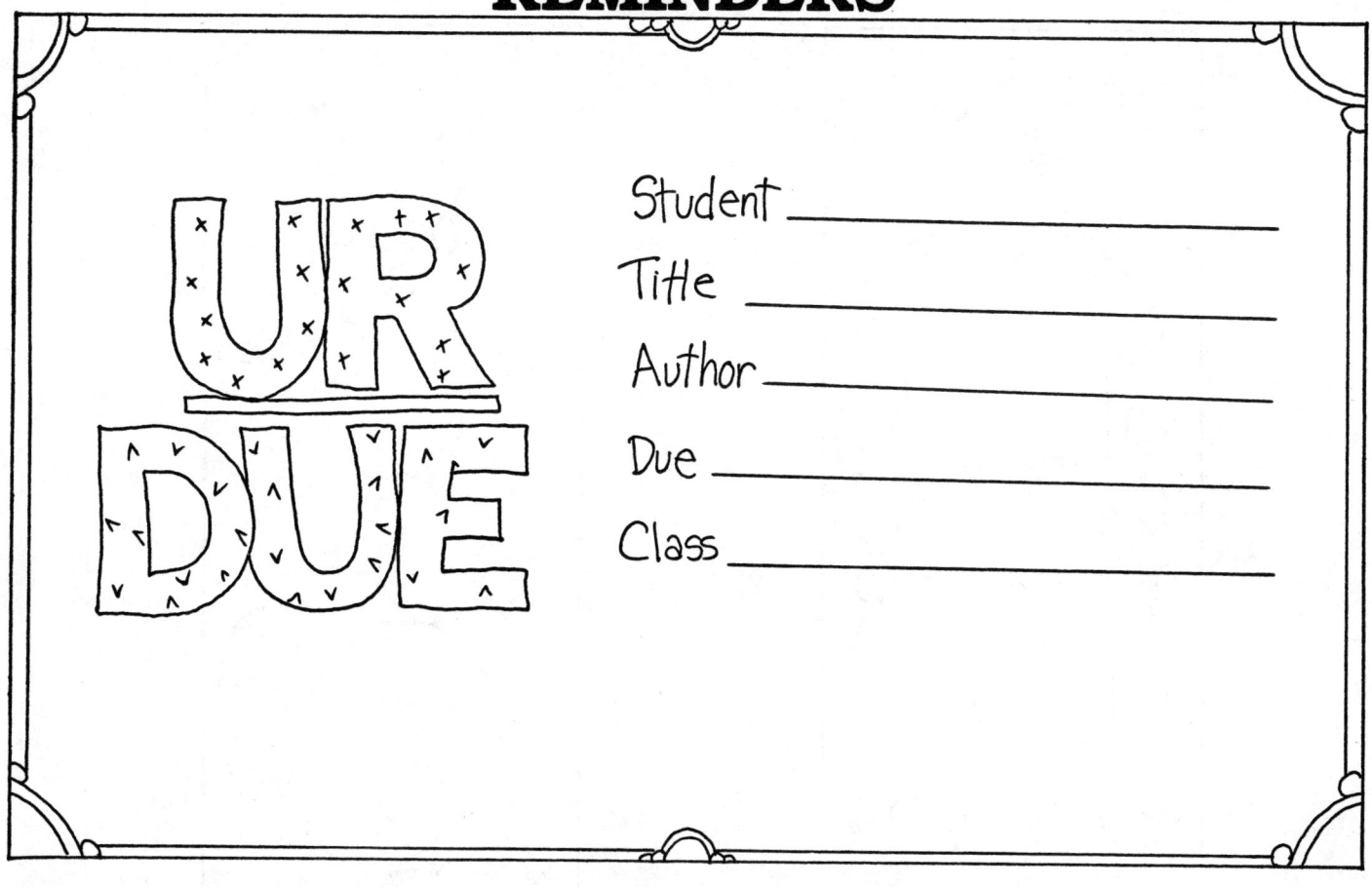

UR DUE

Student _____
Title _____
Author _____
Due _____
Class _____

You're Long Overdue!

Student _____ Per. ____
Title _____
Author _____
Due _____ Teacher _____

©1984 INCENTIVE PUBLICATIONS, Inc., Nashville, TN. All rights reserved.

Treat yourself to a good book!

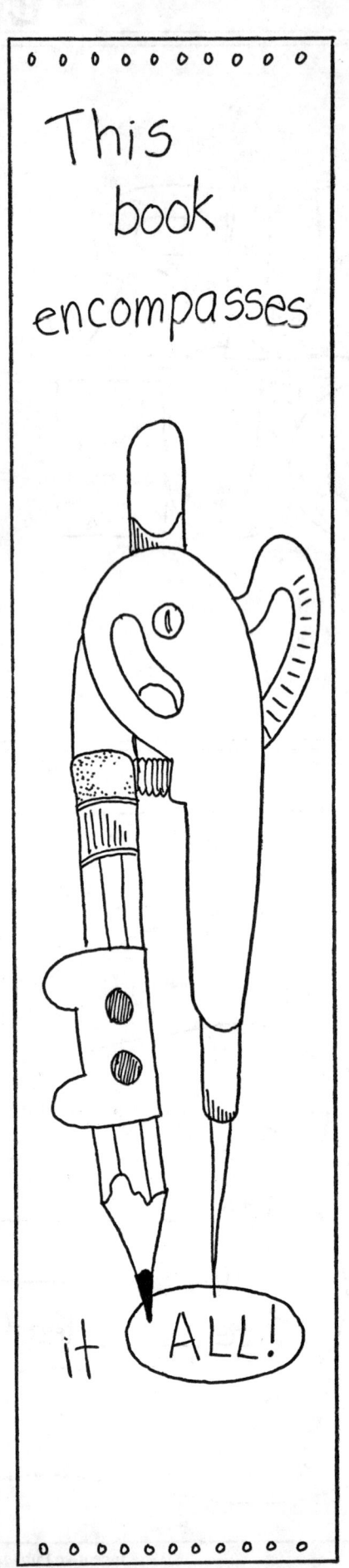

This book encompasses it ALL!

©1984 Incentive Publications, Inc., Nashville, TN. All rights reserved.

I'm Reading Lickety-Split

This Book Sweeps Me Off My Feet

©1984 Incentive Publications, Inc., Nashville, TN. All rights reserved.

This is the best book I ever SAW!

I've got the JUMP on reading

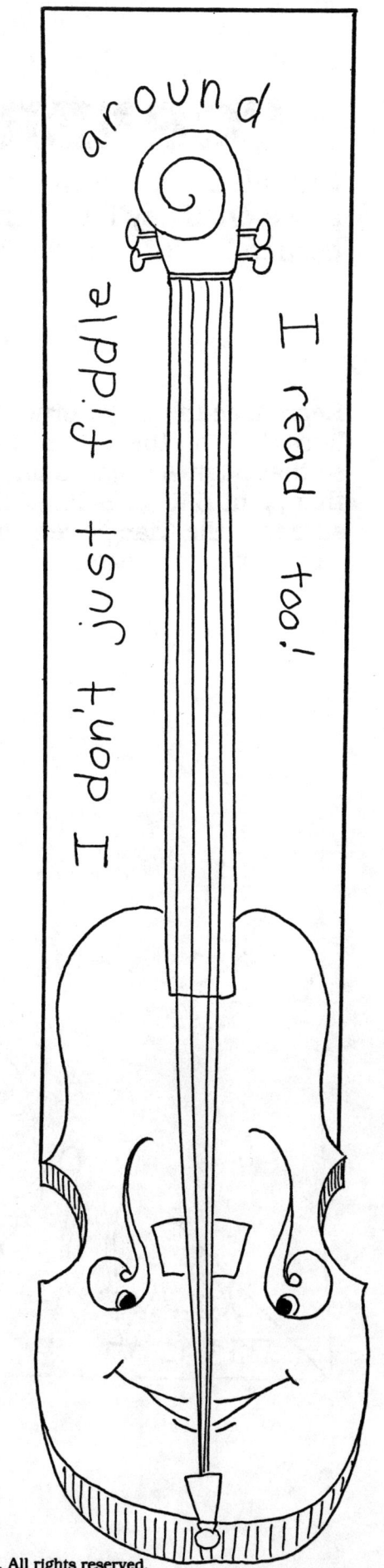

©1984 Incentive Publications, Inc., Nashville, TN. All rights reserved.

CORNER A GOOD BOOK

Cut a few corners and turn out bookmarks your kids can get an angle on. They'll love making and decorating these nifty page corners!

Directions

Reproduce the page corners on duplicating paper. Cut out along dotted lines. Fold on the solid black line toward the back (away from the picture) so that point A touches line CD. Fold on the second solid black line so that point B touches line CD. Secure the top flap to the bottom flap. Make sure that the triangle remains open along the bottom edge to fit on the corner of a book page.

©1984 Incentive Publications, Inc., Nashville, TN. All rights reserved.

Look whooo's reading!

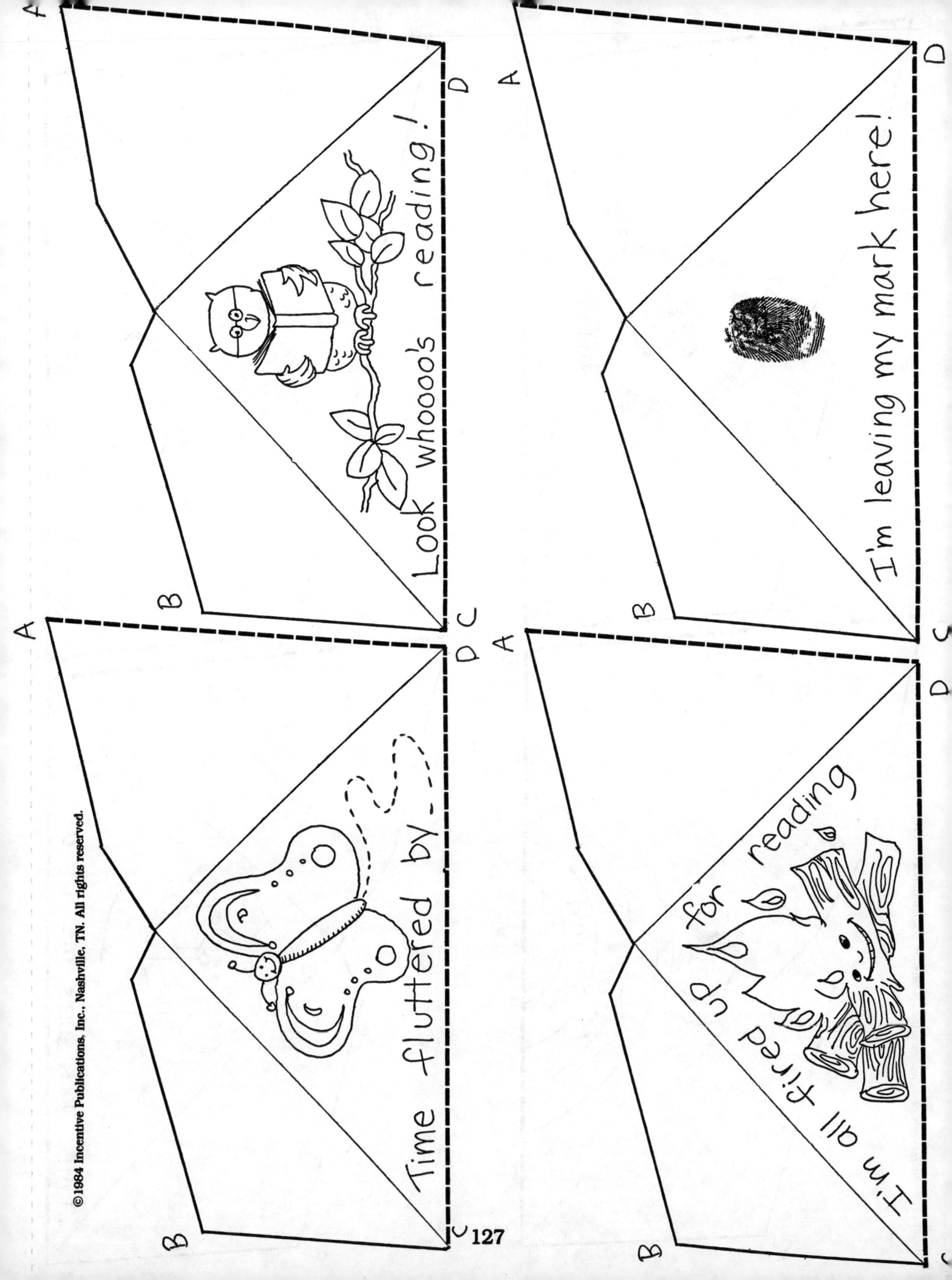

I'm leaving my mark here!

Time fluttered by!

I'm all tired up for reading

©1984 Incentive Publications, Inc., Nashville, TN. All rights reserved.

127

This book makes the mark

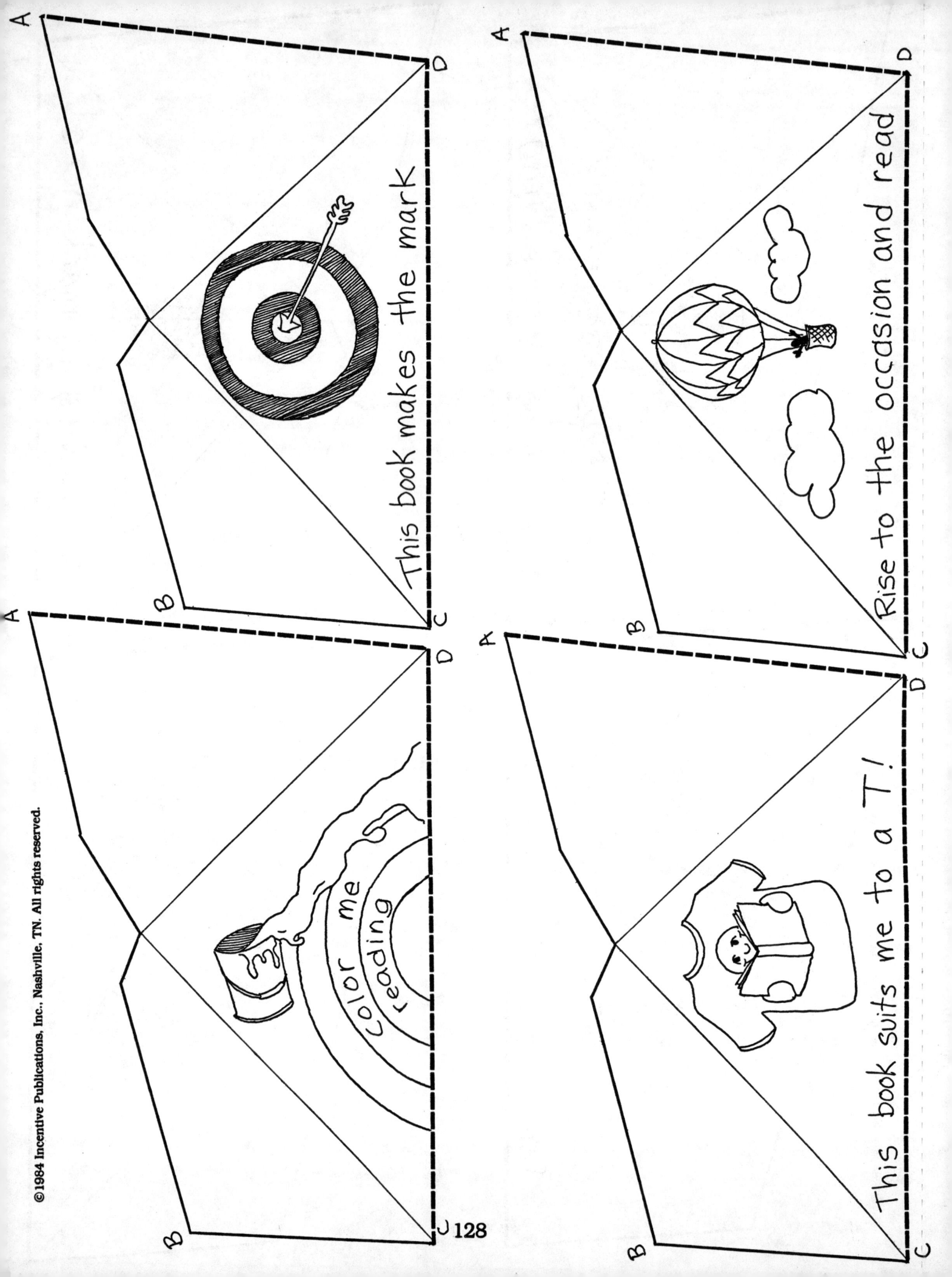

Rise to the occasion and read

This book suits me to a T!

color me reading

©1984 Incentive Publications, Inc., Nashville, TN. All rights reserved.

128